Autism and Managing Anxiety

This easy-to-use resource is a compilation of theoretical background and concrete approaches designed to increase understanding and outline strategies to support autistic children and young people who experience anxiety in the school environment. This resource also has practical application for parents, carers and professionals across a range of educational and community-based settings.

Using real life examples and case studies, the book explains and explores the different forms of anxiety and their impact across the school environment. Each chapter offers practical information and strategies that may help reduce the negative symptoms of anxiety and help support emotional resilience across home and school environments.

Key features of this book include:

- Chapters aimed at enhancing the understanding of anxiety in autism, considering potential triggers of anxiety, discussion on cognitive theories, social communication and means of assessing anxiety.
- A wealth of downloadable anxiety management strategies and resources that can be adapted and used by a teacher, parent or other professional.

This resource has been developed by the multidisciplinary team at **Middletown Centre for Autism**, and is a useful resource for the busy parent, teacher and other professionals who wish to provide individualised support strategies for anxiety across a range of settings.

The all-Ireland Middletown Centre for Autism was established by the Department of Education, Northern Ireland and the Department of Education and Skills, Ireland to promote excellence in the delivery of specialist education services to children and young people with autism.

The Centre delivers its services across three areas of:

- Learning Support and Assessment

The Centre staff work directly with individual autistic pupils and their school staff and families on a referral basis. The Centre staff accept referrals for whole schools to increase their capacity for the development of an autism competent environment.

- Research and Information

The Centre's research department conducts follow-up with all referred pupils and schools and develops practice-based resources based on this work. The department also conducts research projects and provides supportive resources aimed at enhancing educational practice across the island.

- Training

The Centre delivers an extensive programme of training to parents and educational professionals across the island. The Centre's work also includes a graduate certificate in autism education and a graduate diploma in autism studies and a range of online training sessions.

Further details on the Centre's work can be found at www.middletownautism.com

Autism and Managing Anxiety

Practical Strategies for Working with Children and Young People

MIDDLETOWN CENTRE FOR AUTISM

CENTRE FOR AUTISM

Routledge
Taylor & Francis Group
LONDON AND NEW YORK

First published 2021
by Routledge
2 Park Square, Milton Park, Abingdon, Oxon OX14 4RN

and by Routledge
52 Vanderbilt Avenue, New York, NY 10017

Routledge is an imprint of the Taylor & Francis Group, an informa business

British Library Cataloguing-in-Publication Data
A catalogue record for this book is available from the British Library

Library of Congress Cataloging-in-Publication Data
A catalog record has been requested for this book

ISBN: 978-0-367-50502-8 (hbk)
ISBN: 978-0-367-25033-1 (pbk)
ISBN: 978-0-429-28565-3 (ebk)

Typeset in Bembo
by River Editorial Ltd, Devon, UK

Visit the Companion Website: www.routledge.com/cw/speechmark

For Product Safety Concerns and Information please contact our EU representative:
GPSR@taylorandfrancis.com
Taylor & Francis Verlag GmbH, Kaufingerstraße 24, 80331 München, Germany

Contents

List of tables . . . viii
List of resources . . . ix
List of contributors . . . x
Colour coding for visual supports . . . xi
Preface . . . xii

1 Autism and anxiety . . . 1
Introduction . . . 1
Autism . . . 1
Prevalence of anxiety in autism . . . 2
Causes of anxiety in autism . . . 3
Triggers for anxiety in autism . . . 5
Responses to anxiety . . . 6
Autism and anxiety in females . . . 9
Conclusion . . . 10
References . . . 10

2 Social communication, autism and anxiety . . . 12
Introduction . . . 12
Social communication styles in autism . . . 12
Receptive language skills and non-verbal communication . . . 14
Expressive language skills and using non-verbal communication . . . 15
Social skills and social anxiety . . . 17
Cyclical nature of anxiety and communication skills . . . 21
Conclusion . . . 22
References . . . 22

3 Cognitive theories, learning style, autism and anxiety . . . 25
Introduction . . . 25
Theory of Mind (ToM) . . . 25
Self-regulation . . . 27
Alexithymia and autism . . . 27
Double empathy . . . 27
Executive function . . . 28
Working memory . . . 29
Cognitive flexiblity . . . 29
Visual learning style . . . 33
Conclusion . . . 34
References . . . 35

4 Sensory processing, autism and anxiety 36
Introduction 36
Sensory processing and autism 37
Hyper-reactivity 38
Hypo-reactivity 39
Impact of sensory processing on anxiety in autism 40
Sensory triggers for anxiety 41
Behavioural responses to sensory input 44
Conclusion 47
References 47

5 Assessment of anxiety 48
Introduction 48
Formal assessments 49
Informal assessments 50
Assessment of anxiety in autism 51
Assessment measures 53
Conclusion 55
References 55

6 Anxiety management strategies for autistic children and young people 58
Introduction 58
Section one 59
Removal of the trigger 59
Flexibility 60
Communication 60
Formalised approaches 61
Structured teaching 61
Story-based interventions and social communication 64
Social Stories™ *64*
Comic strip conversations *65*
Environmental and sensory strategies 66
Creating a low arousal environment *66*
Calm breaks *68*
Proprioceptive activities *70*
Weighted items *70*
Ear defenders *71*
Graded exposure or desensitisation *71*
Stress kits *72*
Relaxation and mindfulness 74
Progressive muscle relaxation 74
Calm breathing 74
Mindfulness-based activities 75
Adapting mindfulness for autism *75*
Mindful grounding activity *76*
Body scan *77*
Mindful breathing *77*
Guided imagery/visualisation *77*

The happiness switch . . . 77
Section two . . . 78
    How does CBT work? . . . 78
    CBT in autism . . . 78
        Coping statements . . . *82*
Self-regulation . . . 82
Affective education . . . 83
Recognising emotions . . . 83
Identifying anxiety and levels of distress . . . 85
Communicating anxiety . . . 86
    Emotion thermometers . . . 87
    Emotion ladder or traffic light . . . 87
    Incredible 5-Point scale . . . 88
    Self prompt regulation cards . . . 88
Co-regulation . . . 89
    Identifying triggers . . . 89
    Identifying emotions . . . 89
    Regulation of emotions . . . 90
Conclusion . . . 90
References . . . 91

Resources . . . 93
Index . . . 124

Tables

1.1 Diagnostic features of autism 2
4.1 The sensory systems. 36
4.2 Common sensory triggers for anxiety 42
6.1 Creating a low arousal environment 67
6.2 Potential benefits of mindfulness for autistic children and young people 76

Resources

1 Visual schedule for school . . . 93
2 Break out cards . . . 94
3 Calm corner tokens . . . 95
4 Muscle relaxation step by step . . . 96
5 Relaxation breathing . . . 97
6 Square breathing . . . 101
7 Star breathing . . . 102
8 Ocean breaths, rainbow breaths and butterfly breaths . . . 103
9 Count 1–10 . . . 106
10 Body scan . . . 107
11 Feelings thermometer . . . 108
12 Feelings speedometer . . . 110
13 Feelings chart . . . 111
14 Looks/Sounds like rating scale . . . 112
15 Feelings volcano . . . 113
16 Traffic lights . . . 114
17 How am I feeling? . . . 115
18 When I am frustrated . . . 116
19 When I need help . . . 118
20 Anger management cards . . . 120
21 How do I feel? . . . 121
22 Chill skills for younger children . . . 122

List of Contributors

Sheila Cross
Research Projects Manager, Middletown Centre for Autism

Dr Rachel Ferguson
Researcher, Middletown Centre for Autism

Carolyn Frazer
Autism Intervention Specialist and Speech and Language Therapist, Middletown Centre for Autism

Dr Fiona McCaffrey
Head of Research and Development, Middletown Centre for Autism

Jill McCanney
Autism Trainer/Advisor and Specialist Occupational Therapist, Middletown Centre for Autism

Tara McGowan
Specialist Teacher, Middletown Centre for Autism

Eimear McSherry
Technical Officer, Middletown Centre for Autism

Edel Quinn
Autism Trainer/Advisor and Cognitive Behavioural Therapist, Middletown Centre for Autism

Colour coding for visual supports

Communication – red

Calming techniques – blue

Emotional regulation – green

Visual prompt – yellow

Visual support	**Category**	**Colour**
Resource 1 Visual schedule for school	Communication	red
Res 2 Break out cards	Communication	red
Res 3 Calm corner tokens	Communication	red
Res 4 Muscle relaxation step by step	Calming techniques	blue
Res 5 Relaxation breathing smell flowers	Calming techniques	blue
Res 6 Square breathing	Calming techniques	blue
Res 7 Star breathing	Calming techniques	blue
Res 8 Ocean breaths, rainbow breaths and butterfly breaths	Calming techniques	blue
Res 9 Count 1-10	Calming techniques	blue
Res 10 Body scan	Calming techniques	blue
Res 11 Feelings thermometer	Emotional regulation	green
Res 12 Feelings speedometer	Emotional regulation	green
Res 13 Feelings chart	Emotional regulation	green
Res 14 Looks/Sounds like rating scale	Emotional regulation	green
Res 15 Feelings volcano	Emotional regulation	green
Res 16 Traffic lights	Communication	red
Res 17 How I am feeling?	Emotional regulation	green
Res 18 When I am frustrated	Visual prompt	yellow
Res 19 When I need help	Visual prompt	yellow
Res 20 Anger management cards	Visual prompt	yellow
Res 21 How do I feel?	Communication	red
Res 22 Chill skills for younger children	Calming techniques	blue

Preface

Middletown Centre works across Northern Ireland and Ireland to promote excellence in the education of autistic children and young people; the Centre provides multidisciplinary hands on support on a referral basis as well as full programmes of parental and professional training. The Centre's training is complemented by our research and information service, which produces research and practice-based learning resources and online learning programmes.

This is a practice-based resource developed by members of Middletown Centre's multidisciplinary team including professionals with backgrounds in Teaching, Occupational Therapy, Speech and Language Therapy and Psychology, all of who are currently engaged in supporting autistic children and young people in school, home and community environments. The strategies included, while not exhaustive, are grounded in the Centre's current work supporting anxious children and are evidenced both in research and practice as effective for promotion of positive responses to anxiety and building emotional resilience.

The chapters include visual examples and templates that can be downloaded for use as well as case studies and practice points that enhance the practical nature of this resource; each chapter can be viewed as a standalone resource or the book can be consulted in its totality as a comprehensive guide.

Anxiety is a significant challenge that faces autistic children in the school system, and while there are no quick-fix or one-stop solutions it is the Centre's hope this resource will provide the foundations of an individualised anxiety support programme that is based on assessment and that continues to evolve with the autistic student as they engage in family, school and community life.

1. Autism and anxiety

Introduction

Anxiety is a common response to stressors experienced throughout life, such as starting a new school, taking examinations or moving house. In some circumstances, anxiety can be helpful as it triggers adrenaline responses which help the brain and body to cope with the stressors. These adrenaline responses help individuals to run from danger, enhance cognitive functioning in an examination or improve motivation to complete a challenging task. Prolonged and frequent anxiety, however, is physically and emotionally damaging as the body needs time to recover and repair after adrenaline releases. A person who has persistent and pervasive anxiety does not have the opportunity to recover and the impact on mental health can be significant.

Anxiety is a prevalent problem for autistic children (White and Roberson-Nay, 2009; Ozsivadjian and Knott, 2011), affecting at least 40% of individuals who have a diagnosis of autism (Van Steensel et al., 2011). The impact of anxiety on school-age children with autism is significant, adversely affecting school attendance, educational attainment, family quality of life and parental stress (Dabrowska and Pisula, 2010; Carter et al., 2013).

Autism

Autism is characterised by a spectrum of differences categorised in diagnostic criteria as difficulties in social communication, and restricted, repetitive interests and behaviours (American Psychiatric Association (APA), 2013; World Health Organisation (WHO), 2018). The Diagnostic and Statistical Manual (5th edition) (DSM-5) (APA, 2013) provides criteria for a diagnosis of autism and lists examples of how these criteria may be observed. Examples of the criteria are provided in Table 1.1.

The criteria set out in DSM 5 (APA, 2013) and in the International Classification of Diseases (11th edition) (ICD-11) (WHO, 2018) also highlight that for a diagnosis to be confirmed, autistic features must have been present in early development and significantly impact current functioning.

These autistic features can often become predisposing factors for anxiety, placing autistic children at a higher risk of developing anxiety.

Table 1.1 Diagnostic features of autism

Deficits in social communication and interaction
- May not initiate or respond to social interactions
- Lack of reciprocity in conversations
- Unusual eye contact and body language
- Difficulties understanding gestures
- May not adjust behaviour appropriately to context
- Lack of engagement in imaginative play
- Difficulty in forming and maintaining friendships

Restricted and repetitive interests and behaviours
- Stereotypes or repetitive movements and/or speech
- Insistence on sameness
- Strict adherence to routines
- Anxiety in response to small changes
- Strong attachment to favourite objects
- Extremely fixated and restricted interest on a topic, activity or object
- Hyper-reactivity or hypo-reactivity to sensory input, or an unusual preoccupation with specific sensory input

Point to remember

Every autistic child will have a unique set of differences and strengths and they will all be affected by their autism in different ways. A flexible approach to their specific needs and skills is therefore essential.

Prevalence of anxiety in autism

Anxiety is cited as one of the main co-existing difficulties for autistic children (Smith Myles, 2003; White and Roberson-Nay, 2009; Kent and Simonoff, 2017) with up to 84% experiencing anxiety at some time (Ozsivadjian and Knott, 2011). The earliest observations of autism, made by Kanner in 1943 and Asperger in 1944, described autistic children presenting with high levels of worry, obsessions and fear of social encounters (Frith, 1991).

A study by Van Steensel et al. (2011) found that approximately 40% of autistic children have been diagnosed with at least one co-existing anxiety disorder, with the following prevalence rates:

- Specific Phobia: 30%
- Obsessive–Compulsive Disorder: 17%
- Social Anxiety Disorder/Agoraphobia: 17%

- Generalised Anxiety Disorder: 15%
- Separation Anxiety Disorder: 9 %
- Panic Disorder: 2%

The prevalence of anxiety in autism suggests that there is a correlational relationship between them, but causality is still unclear. Kerns and Kendall (2012) suggest that anxiety is both influential to autism and influenced by autism. There are a number of core autistic characteristics which may predispose a child to developing anxiety.

Causes of anxiety in autism

People with autism may be more prone to experiencing anxiety due to biological differences in brain structure and function and due to the core characteristics.

1. *Social communication differences*
   Differences in both expressive and receptive language skills can create high levels of confusion and frustration for autistic children. Interpreting non-verbal cues alongside complex language can be overwhelming, while difficulties in communicating fluently and coherently can lead to anxiety in social interactions. This creates a cycle of negative social communicative experiences, which creates anxiety thought patterns which then further confound communication difficulties.
   Events and people may be perceived as threatening, which exacerbates the anxiety and can lead to withdrawal and isolation.

Case example

Becky is a 14-year-old girl with high-functioning autism. She has an extensive vocabulary and her teachers report that she is able to express herself coherently when asked questions in class. Becky, however, finds it difficult to interact with her peers at break and lunchtimes. She cannot process information when several people are speaking at once and cannot easily contribute to conversations about music, movies and fashion. She has now become anxious at these times and withdraws to a quiet classroom to sit alone.

2. *Insistence on sameness*
   Many autistic children have a strong preference for predictable routines and familiar places and objects. When inevitable disruptions occur, or when introduced to new situations, anxiety often increases. This anxiety can then create an even greater drive for sameness and routine.

3. *Intolerance of uncertainty*

   Intolerance of uncertainty is explained as the 'tendency to react negatively on an emotional, cognitive, and behavioural level to uncertain situations and events' (Buhr and Dugas, 2009, p. 216). People with autism are thought to have a higher degree of intolerance to uncertainty (Neil et al., 2016) and can find uncertain situations, environments or events stressful, which causes negative thinking and can trigger episodes of intense anxiety.

4. *Sensory processing differences*

   Negative reactions to sensory input are common in autistic children. Hyper-reactivity, or over-sensitivity, to sensory input is frequently correlated with anxiety. Many noises, smells, lights, touch and movement are received at a greater intensity by the autistic child, which can lead to sensory overload and anxiety. Unpredictable input, such as a car horn or fire alarm, is particularly stressful. Memories of sensory experiences are stored and affect emotional responses to similar input in the future. The memory of a negative sensory experience is stored and will influence responses to sensory experiences in the future.

5. *Executive dysfunction*

   Executive functions include planning, focusing and shifting attention, initiating activity, self-regulation and impulse control. Some autistic children have difficulty with executive functions and demonstrate functions including impulsivity, disinhibition and difficulty controlling emotions (Ozonoff et al., 1991; Ozonoff and Jensen, 1999; Leung et al., 2015). It will also affect the ability to organise themselves and their belongings. This can limit success in daily activities, such as getting dressed or catching a bus, which can fuel negative thinking patterns and contribute to anxieties. Difficulties in executive functioning also impact on the ability to select and utilise emotionally regulating strategies in stressful situations.

Point to remember

The key features of autism are dually causes and outcomes of anxiety. Differences in communication, sensory processing, executive functioning and a need for predictability can create feelings of anxiety. The anxiety then exacerbates these core differences.

These key characteristics of autism create a world which is confusing and chaotic for an autistic child, and this is further confounded by difficulties in recognising and communicating when they feel anxious, or knowing how to ask for help. The factors listed above predispose an autistic child to developing anxiety, but then there are certain events which can trigger anxiety at any time.

Triggers for anxiety in autism

A trigger is something that causes an individual to feel uncomfortable within their environment, which then creates a feeling of anxiety and subsequent behavioural responses. Major life events like adolescence, illness and death of a loved one can trigger anxiety. Significant changes, such as moving house or starting a new job can also be triggers. Autistic children, however, experience many more triggers, and often on a daily basis. Examples of such triggers may include:

- Transitions: Daily transitions, such as going from home to school, or moving from one activity to another, are often stressful for autistic children. Anxiety is exacerbated if the transition is poorly managed and has not been communicated to the child in advance.
- Unexpected changes to routine: Unpredictability is a significant stressor for many with autism. A substitute teacher in the classroom, the bus arriving late or an activity being cancelled are all examples of changes which can trigger anxiety.
- Unstructured times: When there is no structure in an activity or environment, it feels chaotic and confusing to an autistic child. They cannot make sense of the situation and do not know what is expected of them. Places, such as the school playground or a soft play centre, and activities such as waiting for a bus or free play, tend to increase anxiety.
- Unfamiliar places and people: Autistic children will often become fearful when going to a new place or meeting new people. New toys, clothes and household objects can even cause upset, as there is usually a strong preference for sameness and for familiar objects and places.
- Sensory stimuli: Anxiety may be triggered by specific stimuli which the child dislikes or finds intolerable, or anxiety may be triggered by multiple overwhelming stimuli, which can be experienced in busy and crowded environments. Sensory input can cause even more stress when sudden and unpredictable (e.g. a car horn, a fire alarm).
- Social demands: An expectation to answer a question or to interact with others will often trigger anxiety in autism. This can happen in multiple scenarios throughout the day, including a teacher asking a question in the classroom, participating in a group discussion in school, chatting with friends at a youth club or asking for an item in a shop. The challenges in social communication mean that all social situations can provoke anxiety in autistic children.
- School specific anxieties: The school day presents specific challenges for autistic children. Alongside the typical stressors of exams and homework, there are triggers such as getting to the correct classroom on time, bringing the correct books and submitting homework to a deadline. These demands are particularly challenging for those with autism if they have executive functioning difficulties as any task which requires planning and organisation is stressful. The social communication difficulties associated with autism can also create challenges in the school context as the student may have difficulty processing verbal instructions for a task and does not have the skills to request help. Homework may be recorded incorrectly and information missed. These factors collectively make the school day stressful, leading to a build-up of anxiety.

Case example

Peter is 12 years old and has recently moved to a post-primary school. He has difficulty organising which books to bring to each class and so returns to his locker between every class to collect his books and folders for the next subject. This results in him being late for class and then he is flustered and cannot attend to the instructions, impacting on his ability to carry out assignments correctly. These cumulative triggers cause him to become frustrated and he will often shout at the teachers or run out of the classroom.

Any of these triggers can cause an immediate anxiety response, or the child may try to cope with the stressors, but has an extreme response later in the day. Many autistic children may not recognise their emotions or cannot communicate to others when they are feeling anxious. Emotional regulation difficulties mean that the child may struggle to manage their own responses and to develop coping strategies. When triggers are experienced on a daily basis, with no positive strategies established, negative associations are created which affect the child's confidence and can cause anticipatory anxiety: i.e. a fear of events which have not yet happened. The anxiety can then become a more long-term disorder.

Responses to anxiety

Adults living and working with autistic children need to be alert to the signs of anxiety, particularly as many will not recognise the signs in themselves or have the intent and language to communicate feelings to others. Physiological responses to stressors are often the first indicators that a child is experiencing stress.

Negative thoughts create anxiety about events and experiences, which then cause a perception that the situation is threatening. When information is categorised as threatening, physiological responses are triggered in the brain and body. The sympathetic nervous system automatically sparks nerve pathways to prepare the body for action, while the pituitary gland and the adrenal-cortical system release stress hormones (e.g. adrenaline and noradrenaline) through the bloodstream to prepare the body for a response.

The combined effects of these two systems cause a range of bodily changes to occur, which may include:

- Dry mouth
- Shortness of breath
- Chest pain

- Muscle tension
- Sweating
- Dizziness
- Palpitations
- Blurred vision
- Nausea
- Change in pallor, either becoming pale or flushed
- Dilated pupils
- Shivering

The child may experience physiological responses such as a faster heart rate, nausea, aches and pains, sudden and frequent urges to go to the toilet and changes in breathing pattern.

Point to remember

Children who internalise their anxieties may exhibit physiological indicators, such as sweating, shaking or becoming very pale or very flushed. Children who externalise their anxieties may engage in behaviours such as shouting, aggression or running out of a room.

These physiological responses often lead to behavioural outcomes as the child then reacts to the trigger causing the anxiety. These behaviours are usually the most observable signs of anxiety.

The activation of the sympathetic nervous system and the release of hormones support the brain and body in executing a fight, flight or freeze response to the perceived stress. These behavioural responses are self-protective mechanisms designed to reduce or eliminate the source of anxiety.

- **Fight:** Behaviours may include shouting, hitting out or destroying property. The child may be judged as being intentionally disruptive and aggressive towards others, but when in a high state of anxiety, the child is acting on impulse to self-protect. It may also be the child's means of communicating distress, as functional communication often deteriorates when the child is in a heightened state of stress.

- **Flight:** Behaviours may include running away, withdrawal or refusing to participate in events and activities. These behaviours can be misinterpreted by others as deliberately oppositional, but they are again the child's means of protecting themselves against perceived stressors. If an activity or an event is creating negative emotions, it is natural that the child will try to remove themselves from the situation or refuse to engage.

- **Freeze:** Behaviours may include not moving or interacting and not engaging in surrounding activity. The child seems to shut down and does not respond to surrounding activity and people. This often happens when feeling overwhelmed by sensory input, social interaction and other demands.

An anxiety indicator which is particularly apparent in autistic children is an increase in repetitive behaviours. The behaviours may become more frequent and intense, and the child may be completely preoccupied by them. Examples include blinking, flicking fingers close to eyes, pacing, rocking, teeth grinding and repeating a favourite phrase or sound. Repetitive behaviours escalate at times of anxiety because the child is attempting to regulate emotions by focusing on familiar input in order to block out sources of stress. The repetition is also comforting because it tends to be rhythmic and offers predictability when everything else around the child seems unpredictable.

Case example

Andy is a 10-year-old autistic boy. His classroom assistant has observed that every time Andy has to leave his classroom to go to a different room he counts from one to ten repeatedly while clicking his fingers close to eyes. When she introduced a visual schedule incorporating photographs of the different rooms, these behaviours decreased.

Some children will respond immediately and very obviously to anxiety triggers, but others will internalise their emotions and may suppress the anxiety for long periods. Many autistic children do not want to be seen as 'different' or more anxious than their peers. They do not want to be engaging in obvious displays of anxiety such as running out of a room, refusing to comply or hitting out (Lipsky, 2011). The anxiety then emerges later in the form of extreme responses. The child may be very upset when coming home from school each day as they have tried to cope with stressors, but release the pent-up anxiety when in the comforting home environment. Others may internalise their feelings for days or weeks, and then there may be a sudden emotional outburst. Internalising anxiety can lead to long-term behavioural changes which may not be immediately observed, but can be damaging to both physical and mental health:

- Social withdrawal and isolation
- Reduction in school attendance; school refusal
- Low motivation in daily tasks, including personal care activities
- Development of irrational fears
- Compulsive behaviours (e.g. excessively checking locks, washing hands)

- An over- reliance on alcohol and/or drugs
- Over, under or selective eating
- New or recurrent bed-wetting
- Sleep disturbances and nightmares
- Self-harm
- Negative views, opinions and talking
- Overwhelmed by worry
- Seeks excessive reassurance
- Extreme attachment to an object or person

Adults around the child need to be observant of any of these physical or behavioural indicators of anxiety and respond appropriately. Assessment of the triggers is essential to understand the causes of the child's anxiety and to allow the development of individualised proactive and reactive strategies.

Autism and anxiety in females

Females with autism will present with many of the same core characteristics as autistic males. Their social communication skills will be different from their neurotypical counterparts, they are likely to have sensory processing differences and they will have some level of cognitive inflexibility, restricted interests and repetitive behaviours. There is growing acknowledgement, however, that there are many differences between autistic males and females, and many of the features which are common in girls can be causes of anxiety.

Autistic females often have more social awareness than autistic males, and so may be more perceptive of their differences when they compare themselves to their peers. This awareness of difference can itself create anxiety and then many of these girls have a desire to fit in and be accepted by their peers. They place pressure on themselves to be more like others, but the effort to adapt social behaviours in this way requires conscious effort, which over prolonged periods, causes stress. The effort to fit in will not always be successful, and so girls may experience social failures, which create negative experiences and further anxiety.

Research indicates that girls are more likely to internalise emotions, whereas boys will externalise their emotions through observable behaviours, such as aggression or a refusal to engage (Baldwin and Costley, 2016). An autistic girl is less likely to engage in such behaviours, and may instead exhibit more subtle signs of anxiety, such as a strong attachment to a favourite toy or more discreet repetitive behaviours such as fiddling with hair or thumb sucking. Internalising emotions means that her anxiety may be overlooked by others and so she is not offered help and support (Gould and Ashton-Smith, 2011). This often leads to long-term anxiety.

Females with autism are at a higher risk of being undiagnosed or misdiagnosed (Kreiser and White, 2014). They do not always present in the same way as autistic males and their characteristics may be misinterpreted as something else, such as learning difficulties, personality disorders, obsessive–compulsive disorder or eating disorders such as anorexia (Rivet and Matson, 2011). The differing presentations, between males and females, has resulted in a consistently higher rate of males diagnosed with autism (Halladay et al., 2015) with a reported diagnostic rate of 1 in 42 boys compared to 1 in 189 girls (Christensen et al., 2016).

Point to remember

Many autistic females are not diagnosed until they are teenagers or young adults, and often it is their anxiety which is the first indicator that assessment, diagnosis and support is required.

Prior to diagnosis, they may be acutely aware of their differences but do not know why they feel and act differently to their peers. As they enter adolescence, social and academic demands increase, and there are hormonal and physical changes to their bodies. These factors can lead to an escalation in anxiety. This escalation often prompts the need for assessment and diagnosis, but by then anxiety is already affecting many parts of their daily lives.

Conclusion

Anxiety is not exclusive to autism, but many of the characteristics of autism create a higher risk of developing anxiety. There are stressors which are common to both autistic children and neurotypical children, but there are specific triggers which elevate anxiety in those with autism. Intervention strategies to manage anxiety in autistic children therefore require a tailored approach, individualised to their unique learning style and addressing the underlying causes specific to them.

References

American Psychological Association (2013). *Diagnostic and Statistical Manual of Mental Disorders, 5th Edition: DSM-5.* Arlington, VA: American Psychiatric Association.

Baldwin S and Costley D (2016). The experiences and needs of female adults with high-functioning autism spectrum disorder. *Autism, 20*, 483–95.

Buhr K and Dugas MJ (2009). The role of fear of anxiety and intolerance of uncertainty in worry: An experimental manipulation. *Behaviour Research and Therapy, 47*, 215–23.

Carter EW, Harvey MN, Taylor JL and Gotham K (2013). Connecting youth and young adults with autism spectrum disorders to community life. *School Psychology, 50*, 888–98.

Christensen DL, Baio J, Van Naarden Braun BK, Bilder D, Charles J, Constantino JN, Daniles J, Durkin MS, Fitzgerald RT, Kurzius-Spencer M, Lee LC, Pettygrove S, Robinson C, Schulz E, Wells C, Wingate MS, Zahorodny W and Yeargin-Allsopp M (2016). Prevalence and characteristics of autism spectrum disorder among children aged 8 years–Autism and developmental disabilities monitoring network, 11 sites, United States, 2012. *Morbidity and Mortality Weekly Report Suveillance Summaries, 65*, 1–23.

Dabrowska A and Pisula E (2010). Parenting stress and coping styles in mothers and fathers of pre-school children with autism and down syndrome. *Journal of Intellectual Disability Research, 54*, 266–80.

Frith U (1991). *Autism and Asperger Syndrome*. Cambridge, UK: Cambridge University Press.

Gould J and Ashton-Smith J (2011). Missed diagnosis or misdiagnosis? Girls and women on the autism spectrum. *Good Autism Practice, 1*, 34–41.

Halladay AK, Bishop S, Constantino JN, Daniles AM, Koenig K, Palmer K, Messinger D, Pelphrey K, Sanders SJ, Singer AT, Taylor JL and Szatmari P (2015). Sex and gender differences in autism spectrum disorder: Summarizing evidence gaps and identifying emerging areas of priority. *Molecular Autism, 6*, 1–5. Article no. 36.

Kent R and Simonoff E (2017). Prevalence of Anxiety in Autism Spectrum Disorders. In Kerns CM, Renno P, Storch EA, Kendall PC and Wood JJ (eds) *Anxiety in Children and Adolescents with Autism Spectrum Disorder: Evidence-Based Assessment and Treatment* (pp. 5–32). London: Academic Press.

Kerns CM and Kendall PC (2012). The presentation and classification of anxiety in autism spectrum disorder. *Clinical Psycholgy and Practice, 19*, 323–47.

Kreiser NL and White SW (2014). ASD in females: Are we overstating the gender difference in diagnosis? *Clinical Child and Family Psychology Review, 17*, 67–84.

Leung RC, Vogan VM, Powell TL, Anagnostou E and Taylor MJ (2015). The role of executive functions in social impairment in autism spectrum disorder. *Child Neuropsychology, 22*, 336–44.

Lipsky D (2011). *From Anxiety to Meltdown: How Individuals on the Autism Spectrum Deal with Anxiet, Experience Meltdowns, Manifest Tantrums and How You Can Intevene Effectively*. London: Jessica Kingsley Publishers.

Myles BS (2003). Social Skills Instruction for Children with Asperger Syndrome. In DuCharme RW and Gullotta TP (eds) *Asperger Syndrome. Issues in Children's and Families' Lives, 3, 21–42*. Boston: Springer.

Neil L, Olsson NC and Pellicano E (2016). The relationship between intolerance of uncertainty, sensory sensitivities, and anxiety in autistic and typically developing children. *Journal of Autism and Developmental Disorders, 46*, 1962–73.

Ozonoff S and Jensen J (1999). Specific executive function profiles in three neurodevelopmental disorders. *Journal of Autism and Developmental Disorders, 29*, 171–77.

Ozonoff S, Strayer DL, McMahon WM and Filloux F (1991). Executive function abilities in autism and tourette syndrome: An information processing approach. *Journal of Child Psychology and Psychiatry, 35*, 1015–32.

Ozsivadjian A and Knott F (2011). Anxiety problems in young people with autism spectrum disorder: A case series. *Clinical Child Psychology and Psychiatry, 16*, 203–14.

Rivet TT and Matson JL (2011). Review of gender differences in core symptomatology in autism spectrum disorders. *Research in Autism Spectrum Disorders, 5*, 957–76.

Van Steensel FJA, Bögels SM and Perrin S (2011). Anxiety disorders in children and adolescents with autistic spectrum disorders: A meta-analysis. *Clinical Child and Family Psychology Review, 14*, 302–07.

White SW and Roberson-Nay R (2009). Anxiety, social deficits, and loneliness in youth with autism spectrum disorders. *Journal of Autism and Developmental Disorders, 39*, 1006–13.

World Health Organisation (2018). *International Classification of Diseases, 11th Revision (ICD-11)*. Geneva: World Health Organisation.

2. Social communication, autism and anxiety

Introduction

Communication involves one person transmitting a message to at least one other person via verbal or non-verbal means. Bogdashina (2004) outlines five essential elements for communication to take place:

1. A sender
2. Someone to receive the message
3. A message to communicate
4. A desire to communicate
5. A mode to send that message, for example through words, sign language, picture exchange or an electronic device.

An autistic person may experience difficulties with any one of these steps, and often several.

Social communication styles in autism

Difficulties in social communication are an integral part of autism comprising one half of the dyad of autism. According to the Diagnostic and Statistical Manual of Mental Disorders (5th edition) (DSM 5) (American Psychiatric Association, 2013), for a diagnosis of autism to be made there must be persistent difficulties in social communication and interaction across multiple contexts, which include social–emotional reciprocity, non-verbal communication and difficulties making and maintaining friendships.

Communication styles in autism range from pre-verbal or non-verbal to those who have language skills beyond that expected for their age. Some individuals may show no desire to initiate or maintain interaction while others may interact but only on subjects which are of interest to them. However, despite this there is a commonality in social communication differences with difficulties in understanding the subtle subtext of social communication, and interpreting facial expressions, tone of voice and body language. Fluent communication requires an ability to analyse all relevant information in order to predict and imagine what other people are thinking and will say next in order to respond appropriately. These skills are known as pragmatic language skills and non-verbal communication skills.

Research indicates that children with autism who have higher expressive and receptive language skills experience higher levels of anxiety (Bellini, 2004; Weisbrot et al., 2005; White and Roberson-Nay, 2009). It is theorised that communication skills correlate to the overall level of functioning, and therefore, those who have greater language skills are more aware of themselves and others and therefore may have more awareness of their differences. This can then create anxiety (Mutsatsa et al., 2006). These findings, however, may also be due to individuals with higher receptive and expressive skills being more able to articulate their anxiety than those with lower language scores (Tsai, 1996). This is supported by Park et al. (2012) who found that functional language skills were more strongly related to emotional problems than structural language skills. This means that the number of words an individual can articulate is not a good predictor of how effectively they can communicate. For example, if someone with a limited number of words is able to use them functionally to ensure their needs are met they are less likely to experience anxiety than those who may have a wide vocabulary but not the ability to use it to serve their purpose.

Case example

Sam obtained average scores in language content subtests of CELF-5. He likes to talk at length about his special interest in trains. However, he does not engage in reciprocal communication and is anxious about new environments as he is unable to request and express his needs.

There appears to be consensus that those who have more communication deficits often demonstrate less anxiety within the autism population (Davis et al., 2011). This trend differs significantly within the typically developing population, so careful examination must take place between the nature of communication difficulties in autism and their impact on anxiety.

Point to remember

Differences in social communication styles within autism can be both a cause and an outcome of anxiety. When an autistic child cannot understand language or communicate effectively, anxiety increases, and then this further compounds social communication difficulties.

Studies are ongoing to analyse the specific communication components associated with autism and their impact on anxiety as this relationship is still not fully understood. This chapter provides an overview of communication features within autism and their potential contribution to the high levels of anxiety reported by this population. This is not an exhaustive examination of social communication but outlines key communication issues to give an insight into the impact of some aspects of communication difficulties within autism and their potential impact on anxiety.

Receptive language skills and non-verbal communication

Receptive language skills refer to the understanding of verbal and non-verbal language. Difficulties in this area can result in confusion about instructions, questions and the expectations of others, which can then create immediate anxiety.

Some individuals compensate for receptive language difficulties by watching others to guess what they are meant to be doing. This strategy is frequently utilised by females with autism who are more likely to imitate the behaviours of others in order to mask their difficulties in receptive understanding (Kreiser and White, 2014). Anxiety may however emerge when there is no social model to imitate or in scenarios where instructions and social interactions are more complex.

There are others who do not imitate those around them and are confused by verbal demands. Anxiety may then be demonstrated through engagement in repetitive behaviours or behaviours that challenge as the child or young person does not understand what is expected of them. Ros Blackburn reported that when she experiences anxiety about the 'mayhem' around her, she engages in finger flicking in front of her eyes, and when her anxiety escalates, she bites the backs of her hand (Blackburn, 2000).

Receptive language skills can often be misjudged. It may be incorrectly assumed that when an individual uses limited spoken language that their understanding is low, and that those with a wide vocabulary have a good understanding of language. This can create anxiety as others may then use complex language including sarcasm or poorly constructed confusing sentences. All of this leads to anxiety and an impact on social confidence.

Case example

Andrew is a 12-year-old boy with a diagnosis of autism. He has a wide vocabulary, especially on topics which interest him. He has recently moved to a post-primary school and staff assume that he can follow the complex instructions in the classroom. It has been noted, however, that he is not recording work correctly and is therefore not completing assignments accurately. Andrew's parents report that he is very anxious each morning and has become increasingly reluctant to go to school.

Those with good receptive language skills may still struggle to get the gist of communication due to issues with attention, slower auditory processing times or difficulties understanding non-verbal communication. Difficulties with attention are common across the spectrum and are some of the earliest signs of differences in developmental milestones (Elsabbagh et al., 2009). Differences include a lack of joint attention and the inability to focus on multiple sources of information at once. This has huge implications for understanding and responding appropriately (Jones, Carr and Feeley, 2006). In the busy classroom, there are multiple sources of auditory stimuli to process, including the teacher talking, the data projector, classmates chatting and traffic outside. This will then affect the ability to process and understand verbal instructions, leaving the young person anxious about what is expected of them.

Research indicates that individuals with autism often have increased processing times for verbal communication (Hedvall et al., 2013), which limits the amount of information that can be understood in real time. Therefore, if teachers talk for a long time without using any visual supports to aid processing and understanding then these individuals are likely to become overloaded and anxious. Studies also show that anxiety then further increases processing time, and so a cycle is perpetuated (Chang, Quan and Wood, 2012). The effects of this will be greater if others speak too quickly or use metaphorical language.

Point to remember

An individual may have an adequate understanding of concrete language but can become confused by more abstract forms of communication, such as metaphors, sarcasm or making inferences. This can then lead to errors in social interactions, which may contribute to feelings of social anxiety.

Understanding and following instructions can also be impacted by literal interpretation of language, ambiguous requests or being unable to interpret tone of voice, body language, context or facial expression. Temple Grandin reported:

> People's facial expressions seemed idiosyncratic contortions. As faces, they were so very hard to recognise because they never remained constant.
>
> (Grandin, 1995, p. 15)

Adam Harris (2015), an autistic adult, reported that he does not know if people are joking or being serious as he has difficulties interpreting tone. Such difficulties can result in feelings of confusion.

Expressive language skills and using non-verbal communication

Expressive language skills refer to our ability to use language in order to communicate effectively. We use language for many purposes including asking questions, expressing our needs and wants, commenting and expressing our feelings. Some young people with autism do not see the need to communicate or understand the power of using language. Others may have the desire to communicate but lack the means to do so, possibly due to motor planning or oral motor difficulties. This can then lead to high levels of frustration and subsequent anxiety, especially if the individual has good receptive understanding and a desire to interact (Bogdashina, 2004). An individual who is experiencing a toothache may have no means to communicate this to those around them. The distraction and distress caused by the pain will prevent the person participating in their daily routines, which may be misinterpreted as noncompliance, the implications of which will further compound the anxiety.

Case example

Daniel is 6 years old and is pre-verbal. At present he has no means in place to functionally ask for things in order to meet his basic needs. At home he climbs to get items he wants from cupboards and opens the fridge to get a drink. When out in the community he will often have episodes in which he lies on the ground and screams, and it can take a considerable length of time for his parents to work out what he needs. During these times he will often bang his head or bite the back of his hand. This causes himself and his parents high levels of anxiety about being out in the community.

Difficulties engaging in functional dialogue can have far reaching implications. It may contribute to a lack of rapport with teachers, for example, which is critical in terms of self-esteem (Sciutto et al., 2012; Dillon, Underwood and Freemantle, 2014). There is a risk that if a young person experiences repeated failure in interactions with peers, they may feel anxious about future interactions, resulting in social avoidance and isolation.

The burden of responsibility does not lie with the individual with autism alone. Time must be taken to learn how the young person communicates and how to support their understanding and means of expressing themselves. Moreover, it is paramount that peers are given training about autism and how best to communicate with their classmate in order to support communication. Adults and those in a supportive capacity should also monitor their own communication styles and ensure that they are communicating in a style and pace that is congruent with the differing communicative needs of the autistic person.

> It is essential to understand the nature of autistic conditions. People with these disorders, because of their social impairments, cannot meet you halfway. You have to make an imaginative leap into their world and try to see things from their point of view.
>
> (Wing, 1996, p. 87)

> right from the start, from the time someone came up with the word "autism", the condition has been judged from the outside, by its appearances, and not from the inside according to how it is experienced.
>
> (Donna Williams, 1996, p. 14)

Often the anxiety level of the young person with autism is overlooked or underestimated due to difficulties in identifying and reporting anxiety. This is prevalent even in those with a high level of expressive language skills. They may have alexithymia and so cannot identify and describe emotions. The expressive language skills of people with autism is often affected when anxious, so an individual who is usually articulate may lose the ability to describe feelings or ask for help when under stress.

Point to remember

Interaction is typically expected to happen in social contexts such as the school playground, a birthday party, a restaurant or the sports club. These are noisy and busy environments with multiple conversations happening simultaneously. This is then likely to increase anxiety levels in the person with autism and affects their ability to participate in interactions.

Anxiety levels should not be judged based on facial expressions, as research demonstrates that facial expressions may not be a good gauge of the internal state of the autistic person (Guha et al., 2015). Those supporting individuals with autism should instead be cognisant of physiological signs of anxiety and changes in behavioural patterns, such as an increase in repetitive behaviours. Professionals and those working in a supportive capacity should work with the autistic student to provide ways of understanding and communicating their internal state.

Social skills and social anxiety

Social cognition refers to a number of cognitive processes which guides us in what to say and do in specific social situations (Happé, Cook and Bird, 2017). Each social situation is unique and unpredictable, meaning it is difficult to apply rules from one social setting to another. For example, telling an inappropriate joke to your peers might make them laugh, but a student would get a very different reaction from the School Principal. Instead, social cognition allows us to automatically and unconsciously analyse social situations in order to respond in an expectant way. Individuals with autism display difficulties in this area, placing them at risk of making social mistakes which in turn may lead to negative social responses. This impacts on the ability to make and maintain friendships. Girls may be particularly harshly judged, as the expectation is that they should be more empathetic and sensitive than boys (Davis and Wilson, 2016).

> … I know we are there to learn, but there seems to be so much more going on than that. It is like beginning a game without knowing any of the rules or passwords …
>
> (Luke Jackson, 2002)

Research findings show that like their peers, autistic young people seek friendship and connections (Bauminger et al., 2008; Daniel and Billingsley, 2010), but many experience difficulties making and maintaining friendships and consequently navigate the social world without close friendships (Koning and Magill-Evans, 2001). This mismatch between wanting friendships but being unable to cope with the behaviour of others at times can cause anxiety. There is also a high likelihood of negative social experiences such as communication breakdown, peer rejection, bullying or social isolation which will have an impact on mental health.

> The difficulties of trying to communicate effectively, fit in socially, and navigate their own and others' emotions are enough to cause an extraordinary degree of stress in many (young people with Autism).
>
> (McAfee, 2001, p. 3)

Some young people state that they do not want friendships, which is often due to a high number of previous negative experiences. This reduces motivation for the young person to initiate communication or to develop social skills. Moreover, it may result in young people looking for friendships which are inappropriate, through online forums, for example. However, it is important to note that even though individuals may want social connections, they may need time to be on their own to self-regulate and calm.

Case example

James is 15 and attends a mainstream secondary school. He is very bright academically but struggles to understand the intentions and perspectives of others. He takes language literally and gets frustrated when things happen which he does not expect. When he becomes overwhelmed, he needs to be alone and seeks to remove himself from the classroom. Staff are worried about him and so follow him, trying to engage in interaction with the intention of helping him. For James this compounds his feelings of anxiety and results in him trying to run away from staff.

Repeated negative social experiences can place individuals with autism at risk of developing social anxiety where there is anticipatory anxiety about future social situations, (Spain et al., 2017). Studies suggest that if an individual experiences high levels of physiological arousal when faced with negative social experiences, then they are most at risk of developing social anxiety (Bellini,

2006). In such instances, the young person's 'fight or flight' response is triggered, which results in anticipatory anxiety about future social situations. Social anxiety therefore is described as having an excessive and persistent fear of social and/or performance situations such as school, parties, leisure activities and more. Individuals with social anxiety often engage in negative thinking patterns. Within a school context social anxiety means many are reluctant to:

- Contribute to class discussions
- Take part in group work
- Give presentations or answer a question in front of the class
- Participate in extracurricular activities
- Attend social events, such as parties

Point to remember

Repeated negative experiences of social interactions affects the desire to have friendships and impacts upon the ability to make and maintain friendships. Social isolation can then exacerbate anxiety as the person does not have a support network for social situations.

Social anxiety is the most commonly diagnosed type of anxiety with the autism spectrum (Simonoff et al., 2008). Unfortunately, without intervention social anxiety appears to get worse over time, with autistic people reporting isolation and loneliness that increased as their social communication awareness developed (Müller, Schuler and Yates, 2008; Orsmond et al., 2013).

There are two subtypes of social anxiety: those whose primal fear is that of performance and fear of negative evaluation; and those with performance fears along with general social interaction fears (Turner, Beidel and Townsley, 1992). As is typical with social anxiety these students may constantly feel that others are judging their behaviour, which can lead to a great deal of self-consciousness, distress and avoidance. However, social anxiety can occur without the usual fear of negative evaluation (Vasa et al., 2016); instead there are much higher levels of rumination (Crane, Goddard and Pring, 2013). This means the autistic person might replay a negative social scene in their mind over and over again, feeling confused as they do not know what went wrong.

Many young people with autism replay bullying interactions in their mind, feeling confused about why someone would treat them in that way. Often a young person will not know they have experienced bullying at the time due to limited social awareness; however, as their insight grows over time they look back and understand that they were mistreated and experience delayed distress and anxiety (Gray, 2004). Again, this may be particularly common in females with autism as bullying forms within this group are typically subtle and involve complex relational aggression, rather than overt forms such as physical aggression, more typical among males (Card et al., 2008). Social anxiety causes many students to miss confidence-building opportunities, which further cements their fall into a vicious cycle of perpetuating anxiety. Anxiety may lead to avoidance of social situations and therefore limit the individual's opportunities to practise social skills (White et al., 2014), compounding the already present social difficulties and isolation. Fewer friendships and social isolation can lead to negative outcomes such as depression, poor academic performance and school refusal (Whitehouse et al., 2009; Pouw et al., 2013).

Case example

Alex experienced bullying as a young child when she was 5. When aged 15 and speaking to a professional, she recalled every detail of the interactions and cried, asking: 'Why would they do that to me?' Up until this point Alex did not have the social insight to understand that others had intended to cause her harm. She now presents with a high level of anxiety in school settings, in part because of her past experiences of bullying.

Autistic young people may feel particularly anxious about communicating with others during unstructured times and leisure times such as at parties, youth clubs or break time in school. The young person may avoid social interactions by hiding in quiet places such as the toilets. However, being alone in places where adult supervision is low increases vulnerability for bullying (Hebron, 2012).

Social anxiety may also cause a young person to be over zealous in their attempts to make friends and this energy can be misplaced.

Case example

Michelle is a 13-year-old with autism and Attention Deficit Hyperactivity Disorder (ADHD); she attends a mainstream secondary school. Sarah wants social relationships with those in her class but has difficulties in maintaining friendships. She is socially motivated and initiates interaction with others and has developed a number of friendships. However, due to previous social rejection she fears that her friends will stop speaking to her and is too intense in her interactions. When she texts her friends and they do not reply her anxiety that she will lose her friend is evoked and she starts to message them constantly. This is overwhelming for her peers, who will then distance themselves for her. This affirms Michelle's belief that she cannot keep friends and perpetuates her anxiety around keeping friends.

As social skill deficits are a key component in the development of social anxiety, social skills interventions are key to helping young people avoid negative peer interactions which can lead to and compound anxiety. Seventy per cent of young people with autism are educated in mainstream settings (Department for Education, 2014) and peers may not recognise the individual's differences in communication style, resulting in a lack of support from their peers. Therefore, educating peers to be more accepting and teaching them how to interact with individuals with autism is paramount. Peer awareness programmes have been found to improve levels of inclusion and attitude towards students with autism (Campbell et al., 2004; Staniland and Byrne, 2013).

Cyclical nature of anxiety and communication skills

It is also important to consider the impact of anxiety on the development and functional use of social communication skills. Research has indicated that social communication difficulties may be present before an individual develops social anxiety (Pickar et al., 2017). However, this is refuted by other research studies which suggest anxiety present in young children with autism may have a detrimental effect on the development of social communication skills. Davis et al. (2012) found that two years olds with higher levels of anxiety had greater social communication difficulties by age four. Others have theorised that anxiety is also a factor in individuals with autism, with the motor and understanding ability not using any spoken language (Bogdashina, 2004). This is an area that requires further investigation, and at present the impact of anxiety on the development of social communication skills is not fully known. Nevertheless, this highlights the importance of early intervention for anxiety in order to mitigate any potential impact on other areas of the child's functioning.

Research studies have also consistently found that some people's communication skills are inhibited by their anxiety, which then exacerbates their emotional state, and communication is further impacted (Tantam, 2003; Bogdashina, 2004). It is often observed that when a young person enters a heightened emotional state that their speech reduces dramatically. Indeed, it is only when the young person has calmed fully that they are able to engage in two-way communication again.

Moreover, certain communication topics or contexts are more likely to be anxiety provoking and may have a detrimental effect on the young person with autism utilising their communication skills (Johnson and Wintgens, 2001). For example, individuals with autism are more likely to find one-to-one conversations easier as there is less overlap and amount of information to process. When conversations are unstructured and chaotic, such as at mealtimes or in the playground, they are likely to cause anxiety. The young person may deal with this anxiety by trying to dominate the conversation and ignoring the needs of the others, or by becoming quiet and withdrawn. Many parents report that their child with autism has a preference for speaking with adults or younger children, which is often to alleviate feelings of anxiety around communication. Adults tend to provide accommodations to support communication, while younger children are less socially demanding and are more easily led in the conversation, so allow the individual with autism to lead the conversation.

Conclusion

As has been highlighted throughout this chapter, the communication differences experienced by individuals with autism can cause anxiety to build in the moment and also lead to anticipatory anxiety about future social interactions. Many young people with autism do not want to be seen as 'different' or more anxious than their peers. They do not want to be engaging in obvious displays of anxiety or appear as though they are refusing to comply with others (Lipsky, 2011) and so they place pressure on themselves to appear 'normal', further increasing their anxiety levels. It is our responsibility to reduce distractions, pitch communication at a suitable level, teach each individual how to communicate in the best way for them and provide intransient information through visual supports to allow the young person greater time to attend and process the information.

References

American Psychiatric Association (2013). *Diagnostic and Statistical Manual of Mental Disorders*. 5th ed. Arlington, VA: American Psychiatric Association Publication.

Bauminger N, Solomon M, Aviezer A, Heung K, Brown J and Rogers S (2008). Friendship in high-functioning children with autistic spectrum disorder: Mixed and non-mixed Dyads. *Journal of Autism and Developmental Disorders, 38*, 1211–1229.

Bellini S (2004). Social skill deficits and anxiety in high-functioning adolescents with autism spectrum disorders. *Focus on Autism and Other Developmental Disabilities, 19*, 78–86.

Bellini S (2006). The development of social anxiety in adolescents with autism spectrum disorders. *Focus on Autism and Other Developmental Disabilities, 21*, 138–145.

Blackburn R (2000). Within and without autism. *Good Autism Practice, 1*, 2–8.

Bogdashina O (2004). *Communication Issues in Autism and Asperger Syndrome: Do We Speak the Same Language?* London: Jessica Kingsley Publishers.

Campbell JM, Ferguson JE, Herzinger CV, Jackson JN and Marino CA (2004). Combined descriptive and explanatory information improves peers' perceptions of autism. *Research in Developmental Disabilities, 25*, 321–339.

Card NA, Stucky BD, Sawalani GM and Little TD (2008). Direct and indirect aggression during childhood and adolescence: A meta-analytic review of gender differences, intercorrelations, and relations to maladjustment. *Child Development, 79*, 1185–1229.

Chang YC, Quan J and Wood JJ (2012). Effects of anxiety disorder severity on social functioning in children with autism spectrum disorders. *Journal of Developmental and Physical Disabilities, 24*, 235–245.

Crane L, Goddard L and Pring L (2013). Autobiographical memory in adults with autism spectrum disorder: The role of depressed mood, rumination, working memory and theory of mind. *Autism, 17*, 205–219.

Daniel LS and Billingsley BS (2010). What boys with an autism spectrum disorder say about establishing and maintaining friendships. *Focus on Autism and Other Developmental Disabilities, 25*, 220–229.

Davis T and Wilson JM (2016). Gender schema theory. In Naples NA (ed.) *The Wiley Blackwell Encyclopedia of Gender and Sexuality Studies*, 1–3. Malden MA: Wiley-Blackwell.

Davis III TE, Moree BN, Dempsey T, Hess JA, Jenkins WS, Fodstad JC and Matson JL (2012). The effect of communication deficits on anxiety symptoms in infants and toddlers with autism spectrum disorders. *Behavior Therapy*, *43*, 142–152.

Davis III TE, Moree BN, Dempsey T, Reuther ET, Fodstad JC, Hess JA, Jenkins WS and Matson JL (2011). The relationship between autism spectrum disorders and anxiety: The moderating effect of communication. *Research in Autism Spectrum Disorders*, *5*, 324–329.

Department of Education (2014). *Children with Special Educational Needs: An Analysis*. London: DfE Publications. 22.

Dillon GV, Underwood JDM and Freemantle LJ (2014). Autism and the United Kingdom secondary school experience. *Focus on Autism and Other Developmental Disabilities*, *31*, 163–173.

Elsabbagh M, Volein A, Holmboe K, Tucker L, Csibra G, Baron-Cohen S, Bolton P, Charman T, Baird G and Johnson MH (2009). Visual orienting in the early broader autism phenotype: Disengagement and facilitation. *Journal of Child Psychology and Psychiatry*, *50*, 637–642.

Grandin T (1995). *Thinking in Pictures: And Other Reports from My Life with Autism*. New York: Doubleday.

Gray C (2004). Gray's guide to bullying parts I-III. *Jenison Autism Journal*, *16*, 2–19.

Guha T, Yang Z, Ramakrishna A, Grossman RB, Hedley D, Lee S and Narayanan SS (2015). On quantifying facial expression-related atypicality of children with autism spectrum disorder. In *2015 IEEE international conference on acoustics, speech and signal processing (ICASSP)* (pp. 803–807). IEEE.

Happé F, Cook JL and Bird G (2017). The structure of social cognition: In(ter)dependence of sociocognitive processes. *Annual Review of Psychology*, *68*, 243–267.

Harris A (2015). *Autism as a disABILITY*. Retrieved from TED www.youtube.com/watch?v=aPm4cK8FCVw

Hebron JS (2012). *Bullying of Children and Young People with Autism Spectrum Disorders: An Investigation into Prevalence, Victim Role, Risk and Protective Factors*. PhD diss., University of Manchester.

Hedvall Å, Fernell E, Holm A, Åsberg Johnels J, Gillberg C and Billstedt E (2013). Autism, processing speed, and adaptive functioning in preschool children. *The Scientific World Journal*, *2013*, 1–7.

Jackson L (2002). *Freaks, Geeks, & Asperger Syndrome: A User Guide to Adolescence*. London: Jessica Kingsley Publishers.

Jones EA, Carr EG and Feeley KM (2006). Multiple effects of joint attention intervention for children with autism. *Behavior Modification*, *30*, 782–834.

Koning C and Magill-Evans J (2001). Social and language skills in adolescent boys with Asperger syndrome. *Autism*, *5*, 23–36.

Kreiser N and White S (2014). Autism spectrum disorder in females: Are we overstating the gender difference in diagnosis? *Clinical Child and Family Psychology Review*, *17*, 67–84.

Lipsky D (2011). *From Anxiety to Meltdown: How Individuals on the Autism Spectrum Deal with Anxiety, Experience Meltdowns, Manifest Tantrums, and How You Can Intervene Effectively*. London: Jessica Kinglsey Publishers.

McAfee J (2001). *Navigating the Social World: A Curriculum for Individuals with Asperger's Syndrome, High Functioning Autism and Related Disorders*. Arlington, TX: Future Horizons.

Müller E, Schuler A and Yates GB (2008). Social challenges and supports from the perspective of individuals with Asperger syndrome and other autism spectrum disabilities. *Autism*, *12*, 173–190.

Mutsatsa SH, Joyce EM, Hutton SB and Barnes T (2006). Relationship between insight, cognitive function, social function and symptomatology in schizophrenia: The West London first episode study. *European Archives of Psychiatry and Clinical Neuroscience*, *256*, 356–363.

Orsmond GI, Shattuck PT, Cooper BP, Sterzing PR and Anderson KA (2013). Social participation among young adults with an autism spectrum disorder. *Journal of Autism and Developmental Disorders*, *43*, 2710–2719.

Park CJ, Yelland GW, Taffe JR and Gray KM (2012). Morphological and syntactic skills in language samples of pre school aged children with autism: Atypical development? *International Journal of Speech-Language Pathology*, *14*, 95–108.

Pickar H, Rijsdijk F, Happé F and Mandy W (2017). Are social and communication difficulties a risk factor for the development of social anxiety? *Journal of the American Academy of Child & Adolescent Psychiatry*, *56*, 344–351.

Pouw LB, Rieffe C, Stockmann L and Gadow KD (2013). The link between emotion regulation, social functioning, and depression in boys with autism spectrum disorder. *Research in Autism Spectrum Disorders*, 7, 549–556.

Sciutto M, Richwine S, Mentrikowski J and Niedzwiecki K (2012). A qualitative analysis of the school experiences of students with Asperger syndrome. *Focus on Autism and Other Developmental Disabilities*, *27*, 177–188.

Simonoff E, Pickles A, Charman T, Chandler S, Loucas T and Baird G (2008). Psychiatric disorders in children with autism spectrum disorders: Prevalence, comorbidity, and associated factors in a population-derived sample. *Journal of the American Academy of Child & Adolescent Psychiatry*, *47*, 921–929.

Spain D, Sin J, Harwood L, Mendez MA and Happé F (2017). Cognitive behaviour therapy for social anxiety in autism spectrum disorder: A systematic review. *Advances in Autism*, *3*, 34–46.

Staniland JJ and Byrne MK (2013). The effects of a multi-component higher-functioning autism anti-stigma program on adolescent boys. *Journal of Autism and Developmental Disorders*, *43*, 2816–2829.

Tantam D (2003). The challenge of adolescents and adults with Asperger syndrome. *Child and Adolescent Psychiatric Clinics of North America*, *12*, 143–163.

Tsai LY (1996). Brief report: Comorbid psychiatric disorders of autistic disorder. *Journal of Autism and Developmental Disorders*, *26*, 159–163.

Turner SM, Beidel DC and Townsley RM (1992). Social phobia: A comparison of specific and generalized subtypes and avoidant personality disorder. *Journal of Abnormal Psychology*, *101*, 326–331.

Vasa RA, Mazurek MO, Mahajan R, Bennett AE, Bernal MP, Nozzolillo AA, Arnold LE and Coury DL (2016). Assessment and treatment of anxiety in youth with autism spectrum disorders. *Pediatrics*, *137*(Supplement 2), S115–S123.

Williams D (1996) *Autism An Inside-Out Approach.* London: Jessica Kingsley.

Weisbrot DM, Gadow KD, DeVincent CJ and Pomeroy J (2005). The presentation of anxiety in children with pervasive developmental disorders. *Journal of Child and Adolescent Psychopharmacology*, *15*, 477–496.

White SW and Roberson-Nay R (2009). Anxiety, social deficits, and loneliness in youth with autism spectrum disorders. *Journal of Autism and Developmental Disorders*, *39*, 1006–1013.

White SW, Mazefsky CA, Dichter GS, Chiu PH, Richey JA and Ollendick TH (2014). Social-cognitive, physiological, and neural mechanisms underlying emotion regulation impairments: understanding anxiety in autism spectrum disorder. *International Journal of Developmental Neuroscience*, *39*, 22–36.

Whitehouse AJ, Durkin K, Jaquet E. and Ziatas K (2009). Friendship, loneliness and depression in adolescents with Asperger's syndrome. *Journal of Adolescence*, *32*, 309–322.

Wing L (1996). *The Autistic Spectrum.* London, UK: Constable Publishing.

3. Cognitive theories, learning style, autism and anxiety

Introduction

This chapter will address visual learning style and the main cognitive theories which have been associated with autism and will address the following:

- Theory of Mind (ToM) including the double empathy problem
- Executive Functioning (EF)
- Visual Learning Style

Differences in ToM and EF have been associated with a diagnosis of autism and can result in an increase in anxiety. In addition, the preference for visual learning results in anxiety in situations where there is an emphasis on verbal and social communication. This chapter will outline how this visual learning style, when facilitated, can assist in anxiety management.

Theory of Mind (ToM)

ToM refers to the ability to understand the mental state of another individual and therefore predict or anticipate their future behaviours. Simon Baron-Cohen (2000) refers to it as the ability to reflect on the contents of one's own and others' minds. White et al. (2011) refer to ToM as the ability to develop intuitive understanding of one's own and others' mental states and note that there may be a difference in the development of this skill in autistic people.

Social situations and interactions may seem confusing and unpredictable because of differences in ToM. Sharma et al. (2014) note that differences in ToM can lead to feelings of ambiguity in social situations. It means that children and young people may be attempting to interact with others while struggling to understand and predict the responses of others. This can have a significant impact for children and young people as they attempt to navigate a complex social world.

Point to remember

Differences in ToM can affect the ability to understand the intentions and motivations of others. When an adult switches off the computer, the young person may not understand that it is because the adult wants them to move to another activity and may instead think that the adult wanted to upset them.

Differences in ToM mean that autistic children and young adults may have a different style of interaction and a different interpretation of interactions to their neurotypical peers. This can result in stress for them as their communicative and social needs are different and at times may be in conflict with peers. For example, the autistic child may wish to speak about a subject of particular interest while his/her peers wish to play a game with rules that are changeable. The child with autism may not pick up on this differing approach to play/leisure and may feel isolated and excluded as a result. Both approaches to leisure are congruent with the needs of the individual child but the neurotypical child may be more adaptable and read the differences in approach more readily than their autistic classmate. This leaves children and young people at a disadvantage and vulnerable to developing anxiety and avoidant behaviours around social and leisure activities. Without appropriate and individualised support some children and young people can find the understanding of the motivations and experiences of other people difficult to decode.

Case example

Jamie has a great interest in Doctor Who and enjoys talking about Doctor Who with his peers. Sometimes, Jamie's peers want to talk about another topic but they don't explain this shift in topic to Jamie and he doesn't always pick up on the social cues of his peers and adapt to their wishes. This has led to a degree of confusion for Jamie and ultimately anxiety in social situations with his peers, as he does not know how to successfully predict a change in conversation.

In this case example, anxiety could be addressed by providing Andrew with a visual schedule and a timer or countdown to enable him to know when he must transition. Without visual supports such as timers the autistic pupil is left guessing about when he may need to shift attention, which can cause stress and anxiety. Neurotypical children can often draw on the context of the situation to support their understanding of the unspoken rules of the school day.

Case example

Andrew has an interest in the solar system and loves to create detailed drawings of the planets. He is given time to do this each morning but becomes frustrated when his teacher tells him that drawing time is over and he is to transition immediately to the carpet for Circle Time. He finds it difficult to just stop his favourite activity and then to engage in social interactions that are anxiety provoking. This anxiety can escalate into a refusal to transition to the teacher-led activities.

The use of group work is a teaching strategy which is used to make learning more interactive and engaging for students. Usually enjoyed by neurotypical peers, autistic students often find group work difficult due to the potential for unpredictable social interactions in the usually predictable classroom environment. In addition to academic pressures, they now find themselves in a situation where they are required to read body language, facial expressions and predict interactions with peers in a complex, fast-paced social environment.

Self-regulation

In an interview with Middletown Centre for Autism, Dr. Barry Prizant (2012) defined self-regulation as: *emotional regulation achieved independently by an individual* (p. 4). When effectively utilising self-regulatory strategies, a person can achieve a more optimal state of arousal and emotional well-being. Samson et al. (2012) assert that differences in ToM may lead to difficulties with self-regulation. Difficulties with anxiety can follow as a result of challenges with communication and emotional regulation.

Alexithymia and autism

Alexithymia is described as an impairment in understanding one's own emotions and recognising one's own state of psychological or physiological arousal. A person who experiences alexithymia may not fully recognise when they are feeling fear or anxiety. As a result of this, they may not seek support or use strategies to manage their emotions, which can then escalate into angry or upset behaviours. Alexithymia can also have an impact on how the individual processes the emotions of others. Research indicates that autistic people may have an increased likelihood of experiencing alexithymia (Berthoz and Hill, 2005). This additional challenge can further complicate the existence of ToM difficulties and highlights the need for training and support with emotional literacy.

Double empathy

Issues relating to ToM and alexithymia should be considered within the context of what is termed the 'double empathy problem' or a mismatch between the perceptions of the autistic person and the neurotypical person (Milton, 2017). It is not helpful to place the entire communicative burden onto the person with autism and assume that misunderstandings are entirely due to an autistic or related difficulty. Understanding is a two-way transaction and a misunderstanding does not solely lie with one person. In so far as the autistic person may find the neurotypical person difficult to predict, neurotypical people also find the motivations and communication of an autistic person difficult to understand. This is a double empathy problem. It is incumbent upon parents and professionals to take responsibility for their own communications and foster a shared understanding. Cognitive psychology provides some evidence of underlying issues with ToM and recognising and naming emotions in alexithymia. The lived experience of people with autism reflects an experience of being and feeling misunderstood and being discounted on the grounds of having an underlying impairment. It is not helpful to anyone to further isolate the autistic person by assuming any or all communicative issues are due to autism.

Point to remember

Neurotypical individuals have a greater ability to think flexibly and so they should strive to see the world from the perspective of the autistic individual and alter their communicative style accordingly. A teacher can consider the learning style of the student and then present materials in a way which is more meaningful.

Executive function

Executive function refers to a set of developmental abilities which have a significant impact on everyday adaptive functioning and social skills. Executive function is often referred to as the 'CEO' of our brain as it is the part of our brain that helps us to set goals, stay on task and 'get things done'. Executive function is an umbrella term for the following:

- Working memory
- Cognitive Flexibility
- Inhibitory Control

(Hill et al., 2004)

Barendse et al. (2013) confirm that although executive function is not a component of the diagnostic criteria for autism, it has a central role in human development and functioning, and its dysfunction can significantly impact everyday life. Research has shown how the impact of these can lead to a significant increase in feelings of anxiety. Hollocks et al. (2014) note that it is possible that differences in attention in autistic people, controlled by executive function, may place them at an increased risk for developing anxiety disorders. Hollocks et al. (2014) concluded in their study that poor EF was significantly related to greater symptoms of anxiety.

Pellicano (2012) has asserted that the degree of difficulties experienced in relation to EF could play a substantial role in developmental outcomes for autistic children in social competence, adaptive behaviour and success in school, resulting in an increased likelihood of the occurrence of anxiety.

Working memory

Working memory refers to the ability to hold information in one's brain. It plays a pivotal role in attention and learning. Research has shown that working memory may be affected in autistic people.

Barendse et al. (2013) argue that working memory is essential for navigating the complex social world in which we live. It requires us to take in visual and phonological cues, while processing our own and other's emotional cues. They quote Luna et al. (2007) who found a significant difference in working memory ability in adolescents with autism, particularly in relation to social situations. This is at a time when social interactions are perhaps at their most frequent and crucial: the teenage years. This contributes to an explanation for an increase in anxiety during the teenage years.

Case example

Tom has a diagnosis of autism. He attends a mainstream post-primary school. At lunchtime, Tom and his peers go to the canteen. Tom finds it difficult to stand in line for his lunch, process the menu options and contribute to his friends' conversation due to difficulties with executive function. His working memory may not have the capacity to process the above activities, and so he becomes anxious. This can lead to him avoiding the canteen and instead eating his lunch alone in a classroom.

Cognitive flexiblity

Cognitive flexibility is the ability to cope with change and to shift our attention to different tasks or situations.

➢ Coping with change

It has been well documented that autistic people struggle with unpredictable change in their daily lives. Many accomplished adults with autism have spoken about how this difference can impact them on a daily basis. Dr. Wenn Lawson (2017) refers to how cognitive inflexibility can impact his daily life and cause an increase in anxiety levels. His poetry offers an insight into a mind that experiences anxiety and fear in response to unpredictable change:

'change, change and more change,
Of context, place and time.
Why is it that life's transient stage
Plays havoc with my mind?'

Point to remember

Insisting on a rigid routine may be a way of managing anxiety as change and novel experiences can create fear.

Unexpected change can provoke an anxious response, sometimes leading to behavioural responses which can be misinterpreted as resistant or aggressive.

Lawson et al. (2015) found that a diagnosis of autism predicted greater inflexibility, which in turn predicted greater anxiety/depression. It was noted that everyday EF difficulties, such as cognitive inflexibility, were predictors of co-occurring disorders such as anxiety. Individuals with autism need more time to process change and prepare for transitions.

Case example

Jane attends an autism support class attached to a mainstream primary school. Jane was completing an independent task, as was noted on her visual schedule. Her teacher asked everyone to finish their tasks early to go to assembly. Jane was not made aware of this change in the schedule. Jane became very anxious and visibly upset. Jane refused to go to assembly.

In this example, it would have been important to prepare Jane for the change that was to occur during the school day. Jane may have been able to cope with this change and attend assembly with her peers if she had known about it in advance and been given adequate time to process it.

➢ Transitions

Cognitive flexibility allows us the ability to enjoy a smooth transition between activities and events. Difficulty with transitions is something that has been widely associated with autism. Transitions can be divided into macro (big) and micro (small or everyday) transitions. Macro transitions include life events through which many people progress. Life transitions include the transition from preschool to primary school and from primary to post-primary. It also includes the yearly transition through grades/classes in school, i.e. from Year 1 to Year 2. Outside the school context, macro changes may include moving house or the arrival of a new baby at home. Micro transitions are small daily transitions, such as moving from the sand table to the reading area in the classroom or from a maths to a science lesson. It also includes shifting one's attention from completing homework to the table for dinner. Transitions can be a time of great stress and anxiety for autistic children. They are a period of uncertainty and this anxiety can manifest in different ways, depending on age and developmental ability.

Point to remember

Major life changes bring stress for everyone, but they create even greater anxiety for those with autism due to a fear of unpredictable and unfamiliar events. Preparation for change reduces anxiety as it provides greater predictability.

Difficulty with transitions can manifest at different life stages. The transition from primary to post-primary can be a time of anxiety and concern for all children and young people. For those with autism however, it can be a time of significant difficulty. There is a significant change which occurs here in school life and setting, and this can have a substantial impact on the emotional well-being of autistic children.

Case example

Anna attended a small primary school and enjoyed school. She has recently transitioned to a large post-primary school in her local town. She now has many different teachers and must move frequently throughout the day to different classrooms. Anna is finding it difficult to cope with so many micro transitions, along with the added social expectations and interactions that come with her age. She is finding school very difficult, and her mum is finding it more difficult each day to convince her to attend. Anna's anxiety levels are increasing daily and there is a high risk of her starting to completely refuse to go to school.

➢ Sequencing

Executive function controls our ability to follow a multi-step sequence. This is particularly evident in adaptive living skills, such as dressing, making a meal or toothbrushing. Similarly, following a recipe in a Home Economics class or an experiment in a science class can prove difficult for some autistic students. These multi-step tasks require planning and sequencing and often involve locating and organising multiple items. Autistic students who have difficulties with these aspects of executive function are likely to feel overwhelmed and confused in such tasks creating heightened anxiety. The student may forget steps in the sequence or may be missing essential items, further exacerbating the sense of confusion and frustration. This can often initiate a cycle of anxiety in which they experience failure and negative emotions in a task and so become anxious when faced with the task on the next occasion. The use of step-by-step visual supports can assist the student in completing the task successfully.

➢ Planning

Planning and organising are two skills that are very important for successful adaptive living. Autistic students may find it difficult to plan their school day, organise books and follow timetables. At home, they may have difficulty in prioritising homework to meet deadlines or in planning an activity with friends. This may be as a result of differences in their EF. This may become particularly noticeable during the teenage years when young people are required to follow timetables and organise books and resources for multiple lessons while navigating their ways to different rooms. This may serve to increase feelings of anxiety, which may already be present due to the increased unpredictable social interactions which are commonplace during the teenage years.

Case example

Jen has been invited to go to the cinema with some of her friends. She is very keen to join them, but immediately feels anxious about getting there on time, which bus to get and how much money to bring. Her mum helps her to plan the trip, but the bus breaks down on the way there. Jen immediately panics, as she now does not know how to get to the cinema or how to let her friends know that she will be late. She eventually telephones her mum to collect her, but she is now too upset to join her friends at the cinema.

Flexible thinking is an essential component in the ability to solve problems. When presented with a problem, many autistic children have difficulty in finding alternative solutions. Their minds are often compared to single-track trains in that they can perform tasks competently if everything progresses as planned, but if a problem arises, it is like an obstacle on the track and they have no alternate routes around the problem or obstacle. This can then lead to feelings of anxiety as they are unsure of what to do in problem scenarios. In school, they may become anxious if they have forgotten their PE kit or do not have enough money to purchase lunch. Other problem scenarios may include missing the bus when meeting friends or not being able to find items in a shop. Individuals with good executive function can think flexibly around these problems and develop solutions, but many people with autism become anxious when faced with a problem, which further impedes the ability to think clearly and flexibly in order to create solutions. This will then further escalate the anxiety, often causing feelings of panic and fear.

➢ Asking for help

Point to remember

There can be a variety of reasons why an autistic person may not request help. They may not recognise that they are struggling and that another person can be a source of help, and when in a stressed state they may be unable to effectively communicate a need for assistance.

The ability to seek help and assistance from another person is an innate instinct, controlled by our executive function. Autistic children may be unaware that they require help, or do not know how to ask for help or perhaps the engagement of asking for help causes even more anxiety. The student who has not processed the 3-step instruction given by his teacher may be unaware of how to get her attention to ask for help. He may feel anxious and fearful. He may engage in behaviours which challenge in order to avoid the activity as he is unaware of how to request help. Similarly, a student may be aware that he needs help; however, in times of anxiety and stress, the ability to verbally communicate his needs does not come easily and he cannot find the words to express his needs. The use of a subtle, age appropriate visual support to request help can be useful.

Visual learning style

In the early stages of development, two major systems of learning are utilised: explicit learning and implicit learning. Implicit learning typically develops within the first year of life and is necessary for language learning and social understanding. A significant characteristic of implicit learning is that it occurs without conscious attempts to learn. Research studies by Laura Klinger and her colleagues at Division TEACCH suggest that implicit learning in the early stages of development is impaired in autistic children (Klinger et al., 2007). An example of this is that in the first year of life neurotypical babies and toddlers begin to engage in two-way conversations through babbling and imitation of basic sounds. This social skill is implicit and is usually not directly taught by caregivers. Autistic children can also learn this skill, however, more explicit, visual instructions, may be required. It can be hypothesised that when children and young people with autism are required to learn in an implicit manner, they may become confused and unsure of what is expected from them. This can lead to an increase in feelings of anxiety.

Point to remember

People rely on implicit cues to provide clarity. When an autistic person does not pick up implicit information, it can make social contexts very confusing, thus increasing anxiety.

It has been widely accepted that autistic children have a predominantly visual learning style. Temple Grandin, professor of Animal Behaviour at the University of Colorado, speaks about this extensively in her book *Thinking in Pictures*. Grandin asserts that she and many others with autism use visual images to help process and retain information (1995). Grandin states that 'spatial words such as over and under had no meaning for me until I had a visual image to fix them to my memory' (p. 14).

Grandin also tells us that

> when someone speaks to me, his words are instantly translated into pictures … one of the most profound mysteries of autism has been the remarkable ability of most autistic individuals to excel at visual spatial skills, while performing so poorly at verbal skills.
>
> (Grandin, 1995, p. 3)

while Lawson (2017) says 'words without pictures simply go away'.

Case example

Katie is getting ready for school. Katie's mum asks her to put on her coat, find her schoolbag and meet her at the front door. This is a 3-step instruction. Without visual supports, it may take Katie 15 seconds to process the first step and find her coat. She may not have even registered the other two instructions and so does not find her bag or go to the front door. It can appear that she is ignoring instructions, but it is likely that she has been unable to process the complex verbal language without visual supports.

A similar situation may occur in the classroom environment. A teacher may give multi-step verbal instructions, which may lead to a build up of anxiety for the child or young person with autism, as they cannot retain the information and carry out the task. The provision of appropriate visual supports would alleviate this anxiety.

Conclusion

Students who experience difficulties in EF may have weak organisational skills, weak sequencing and planning skills, difficulty with impulse control and poor emotional regulation. Difficulties with ToM may mean children and young people find it difficult to recognise and understand that others can have different thoughts and feelings to their own. The impact of differences in EF and ToM can be very significant and result in anxiety, which can manifest as behaviours of concern in many cases.

The TEACCH model uses structure in the environment and work systems, along with visual supports to help people with autism to live as independently as possible, and addresses these difficulties. This will be discussed in more detail in Chapter 6, which addresses strategies for anxiety management.

References

Barendse EM, Hendriks MP, Jansen JF, Backes WH, Hofman PA, Thoonen G and Aldenkamp AP (2013). Working memory deficits in high-functioning adolescents with autism spectrum disorders: Neuropsychological and neuroimaging correlates. *Journal of Neurodevelopmental Disorders, 5*, 14.

Baron-Cohen S (2000). Theory of mind and autism: A review. *International Review of Research in Mental Retardation, 23*, 169–84.

Berthoz S and Hill EL (2005). The validity of using self-reports to assess emotion regulation abilities in adults with autism spectrum disorder. *European Psychiatry, 20*, 291–98.

Grandin T (1995). *Thinking in Pictures: And Other Reports from My Life with Autism.* New York, NY: Bloomsbury Publishing.

Hill E, Berthoz S and Frith U (2004). Brief report: Cognitive processing of own emotions in individuals with autistic spectrum disorder and in their relatives. *Journal of Autism and Developmental Disorders, 34*, 229–35.

Hollocks M, Jones C, Pickles A, Baird G, Happe F, Charman T and Simonoff E (2014). The association between social cognition and EF and symptoms of anxiety and depression in adolescents with autism spectrum disorders. *Autism Research: Official Journal of the International Society for Autism Research*, 7, 216–28.

Klinger LG, Klinger MR and Pohlig R (2007). Implicit learning impairments in autism spectrum disorders: Implications for treatment. In: JM Perez, PM Gonzalez, ML Comi and C Nieto (Eds.) *New Developments in Autism: The Futire is Today*. London: Jessica Kingsley.

Lawson RA, Papadakis AA, Higginson CI, Barnett JE, Wills MC, Strang JF, Wallace GL and Kenworthy L (2015). Everyday executive function impairments predict comorbid psychopathology in autism spectrum and attention deficit hyperactivity disorders. *Neuropsychology, 29*, 445–53.

Lawson W (2017). *Dr Wenn B Lawson. Poetry.* Viewed in June 2019. www.buildsomethingpositive.com/wenn/poetry.html

Luna B, Doll SK, Hegedus SJ, Minshew J and Sweeney JA (2007). Maturation of executive function in autism. *Biological Psychiatry, 61*, 474–481.

Milton D (2017). *A Mismatch of Salience.* London: Pavilion.

Pellicano E (2012). The development of executive function in autism. *Autism Research and Treatment, 2012*, 1–8.

Prizant B (2012). Autism and emotional regulation. *Middletown Centre for Autism Research Bulletin, No. 8.*

Samson A, Huber O and Gross J (2012). Emotion regulation in Asperger's syndrome and high functioning autism. *Emotion, 2012*, 659–665.

Sharma S, Woolfson LM and Hunter SC (2014). Maladaptive cognitive appraisals in children with high-functioning autism: Associations with fear, anxiety and theory of mind. *Autism, 18*, 244–54.

White S, Coniston D, Rogers R and Frith U (2011). Developing the Frith-Happe animations: Quick and objective test of theory of mind for adults with autism. *Autism Research: Official Journal of the International Society for Autism Research, 4*, 149–54.

4. Sensory processing, autism and anxiety

Introduction

Sensory processing is the ability to receive and respond to sensory input from the external environment and from within our bodies. Dr A. Jean Ayres, who conceptualised Sensory Integration theory, defined it as:

> The neurological process that organizes sensation from one's own body and from the environment and makes it possible to use the body effectively within the environment.
>
> (Ayres, 1989, p. 11)

Sensory input is processed by the central nervous system in a complex sequence which involves receiving, registering, modulating, integrating and interpreting sensory stimuli and then formulating and executing an appropriate motor response.

Sensory stimulation is received through eight sensory systems. Table 4.1 explains the location and primary functions of each sensory system.

Table 4.1 The sensory systems

Sensory system	Location of receptors	Primary functions
Visual (seeing)	Eyes	Seeing colours, shapes, movements, faces, etc.
Auditory (hearing)	Inner ears	Hearing noises, pitches, tones, voices, etc.
Tactile (touch)	Skin	Receiving information about light touch, heavy touch, pressure, vibration. The tactile system can detect danger (e.g. pain) and provides information about the properties of objects (e.g. shape, size, texture).
Olfactory (smell)	Nose	Detecting smells in the surrounding environment.
Gustatory (taste)	Tongue	Detecting different tastes (e.g. sour, sweet, bitter, salty).
Vestibular (movement)	Inner ears	Detection of the pull of gravity and detection of the speed, direction and velocity of the body's movement. Also influences muscle tone and bilateral integration.
Proprioceptive (muscles; body awareness)	Muscles and joints (also tendons and ligaments)	Provides information about body position and the body's movements. Also discriminates the force and pressure of movements.
Interoception	Internal body receptors	Provides information about internal body states, such as feeling hungry, feeling too warm, feeling the need to go to the toilet, emotional states.

When sensory information is successfully processed and integrated, the individual is able to respond in an adaptive way, leading to positive engagement in all daily activities and interactions. Many autistic children, however, perceive sensory input in an atypical way, leading to differences in how they respond to information from their bodies and their surrounding environment.

Point to remember

Engagement in daily activities involves the simultaneous processing of multiple sensory stimuli and integrating these different sources of input to elicit a purposeful response. The brain acts like a computer, inputting the sensory data and formulating appropriate responses.

Sensory processing and autism

Sensory processing differences, while not specific to autism, are highly correlated with autism. Research broadly indicates that at least 85% of people with autism have differences in how they perceive and respond to sensory input (Baum et al., 2015; Tomchek and Dunn, 2007). The sensory processing differences associated with autism are primarily related to how sensory input is modulated. This may also be referred to as sensory regulation, a process in which the brain selects which sensory stimulus requires focused attention, and which stimuli can be ignored. If the brain was to attend to all the multiple sensory stimuli which are constantly received by the body, it would become overwhelmed and the individual may experience 'sensory overload', which can cause distractibility, anxiety and extreme emotional responses. Equally, if the brain does not register adequate sensation to stimulate and alert the brain, the individual will not react to input in an appropriate way, and this affects attention and engagement in daily activities.

Point to remember

The individual selects relevant sensory input and filters out irrelevant input. This process of self-regulation maintains a calm and alert state, which is the optimal state of alertness for engagement in all daily activities.

The Diagnostic and Statistical Manual of Mental Disorders, 5th edition (DSM-5) (American Psychiatric Association, 2013) cites differences in sensory modulation in the diagnostic criteria for autism:

> Hyper-or hypo-reactivity to sensory input or unusual interest in sensory aspects of environment; (such as apparent indifference to pain/heat/cold, adverse response to specific sounds or textures, excessive smelling or touching of objects, fascination with lights or spinning objects).
>
> (American Psychological Association, 2013)

Hyper-reactivity

Individuals who hyper-react to sensory input are sensitive to sensory input. This means they perceive stimuli at a greater intensity and frequency than those with typical sensory processing patterns. Other terms often used to describe hyper-reactivity are:

- Sensory sensitivity or hypersensitivity
- Sensory defensiveness
- Sensory avoidance
- Sensory overload
- Sensory over-responsiveness

Hyper-reactivity is linked to difficulties with habituation. The individual does not habituate to stimuli, meaning that familiar input continues to be perceived as novel and the individual pays more attention to it than required. This can then lead to overload as input is not being inhibited. Neil et al. (2016) link this to intolerance of uncertainty in autism, explaining the theory which postulates that new sensory information is not integrated with past experiences and so everything is processed as new input. Situations then become overwhelming as the individual attends to too much input.

Case example

Jessica goes to a local café every weekend with her family. As soon as she enters the cafe, she is overwhelmed by the noise of people talking, the glasses and cutlery, and by the bright lighting, the pattern of the floor tiles and the smells of the different food items. She also feels uncomfortable with the unpredictable input from others bumping into her while she stands in the queue. She cannot block out all this background input and cannot concentrate on what she wants to eat. She experiences sensory overload and runs from the queue to hide under a table.

Behaviours commonly associated with hyper-reactivity are:

- Distractibility
- Anxiety

- Aggressive behaviours
- Escape
- Shutdown

Hypo-reactivity

Individuals who under-react to sensory input are not effectively registering stimuli and so the brain is not attending to the sensory information from within the body or the surrounding environment.

Other terms used to describe hypo-reactivity are:

- Sensory under-responsiveness
- Hyposensitivity

In hypo-reactivity, too much sensory input has been inhibited and so the brain is not attending to adequate amounts of sensory information. This means that the individual is not in the alert state required for engagement in all daily activities.

This can lead to two different types of behavioural response:

1. *Sensory seeking*
   The individual attempts to increase alertness by seeking out increased levels of sensory input. This may be observed through the following behaviours:
   - Hyperactivity
   - Impulsiveness
   - Fidgeting
   - Creating noise
2. *Low registration*
   The individual is not alert to sensory stimulation and is in a passive state. This may be observed through the following behaviours:
   - Delayed or no response to instructions, questions, name being called, etc
   - Lack of initiation in activities and interactions
   - Disengaged
   - May appear to be lethargic
   - Passive

Individuals may present as hyper-reactive or hypo-reactive to sensory input but are likely to demonstrate a complex combination of both responses, varying across sensory systems and different contexts.

Impact of sensory processing on anxiety in autism

There is extensive research evidence, neurological findings and anecdotal reports which support a correlation between anxiety and the sensory processing differences for autistic people. The correlation most frequently identified is between hyper-reactivity and increased anxiety (Bitsika et al., 2016; Green et al., 2012; Lane et al., 2012). Some research evidence suggests that more severe sensory processing difficulties are associated with higher levels of anxiety (Uljarevic et al., 2016).

A causal relationship has not yet been established. Sensory sensitivities may cause anxiety, but the reverse may also be true. Green et al. (2012) found that high scores in sensory features predicted anxiety, but anxiety was not a predictor of sensory features in children with autism. South and Rodgers (2017) found that atypical sensory processing, alexithymia and intolerance of uncertainty are all predictors of anxiety.

Point to remember

Hyper-reactivity to sensory input is positively correlated with anxiety, and both are also associated with other common features of autism, such as rigidity, insistence on sameness and avoidance of new situations. It is likely that individuals develop rigid routines in order to avoid new or unpleasant sensory stimuli which causes them anxiety.

Sensory sensitivities can be linked to specific phobias. If a child with a tactile sensitivity goes for a first haircut, every touch of the hair and the feeling of hairs falling on the neck may be perceived as painful, and a phobia of the hairdresser is then created. Every time the child returns to the hairdresser, heightened anxiety will be experienced. Black et al. (2017) explain a 3-way relationship between sensory hypersensitivity, anxiety and insistence on sameness, in which an individual becomes anxious in response to certain sensory stimuli and then establishes rigidity as a means of avoiding the unwanted stimuli. A child, for example, may have a tactile sensitivity to soft food textures, which creates anxiety with those foods and then leads to rigidity around only eating the same crunchy food items each day.

There is growing interest in the link between sensory sensitivities, intolerance of uncertainty and anxiety (Neil et al., 2016; Wigham et al., 2015). Causality is again unclear. Intolerance of uncertainty may make individuals more sensitive to stimuli, yet Neil et al. (2016) argue that it is possible that sensory over-responsiveness causes intolerance of uncertainty and increased anxiety.

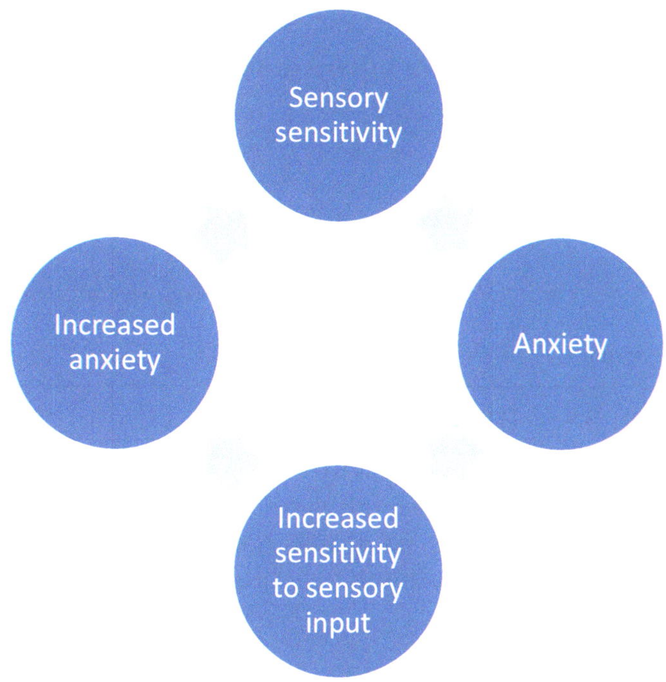

Figure 4.1 'Cycle of Sensory Sensitivity and Anxiety'

The relationship between sensory hyper-reactivity and anxiety may be best understood as a cyclical process, in which one impacts upon the other, creating a continuous cycle of increased hyper-reactivity and increased anxiety. The initial trigger may be a source of sensory input, such as a loud noise or a bright light. In hyper-reactive individuals this can elicit a panic response, and in addition, the input may be associated with an unpleasant memory. This then increases anxiety about the input and stimulates the parasympathetic nervous system, which then further increases sensory sensitivity, and so the cycle is perpetuated as illustrated in Figure 4.1.

Uljarevic et al. (2016), however, suggest that there may be no causal relationship and that sensory sensitivities and anxiety may simply co-occur due to common dysregulation in neural structures such as the amygdala.

Sensory triggers for anxiety

People who are hyper-reactive to sensory input often perceive stimuli at such a high intensity and volume that harmless input can be interpreted as genuinely painful and possibly dangerous. Adam Harris (2015) explains this:

> Every noise, every smell, every texture isn't just something that's unpleasant, it's something that you actually cannot bear.

If input is interpreted as unbearable and potentially threatening, the individual is going to become immediately anxious and stress responses are triggered. South and Rodgers (2017) attribute this to disruptions in the insula cortex, which may cause an individual to overly attend to potentially threatening stimuli and affect their ability to make a reasoned analysis of risk, thus causing heightened anxiety.

The sensory triggers for anxiety will be specific to each individual and can come from a variety of sources.

Table 4.2 Common sensory triggers for anxiety

Sensory system	Examples of triggers for anxiety
Auditory (hear)	Loud noises, e.g. vacuum cleaner Unpredictable noises, e.g. fire alarm Conflicting noises, e.g. simultaneous conversations Constant and high level noise, e.g. at a party, in an indoor play centre
Visual (see)	Bright sunlight Flickering fluorescent lighting Distracting patterns, e.g. on carpet or wallpaper Excessive visual information, e.g. on display boards
Tactile (touch)	Unpredictable physical contact from others, e.g. someone standing too close, accidental nudging or bumping Clothing fabrics and labels Hands becoming dirty Dislike of certain textures and materials Personal care activities, e.g. showering, hair cutting, tooth brushing Engagement in activities such as cooking and painting
Olfactory (smell)	Overwhelmed by some odours Some odours may cause nausea and headaches
Gustatory (taste)	Stress at mealtimes due to aversions to some (or many) foods
Vestibular (movement)	Fear of moving equipment, e.g. swings, roundabouts Fear response when feet are off the ground, e.g. chair/toilet is too high; PE equipment (wall bars, balance beams)
Proprioceptive (body position)	Fear of moving/changing body position. This is more common in individuals with physical disabilities who have atypical experiences of movement and may be dependent on others to move them (e.g. in hoists, wheelchairs etc).
Interoception	Overwhelmed by the multiple internal sensations within the body

1. *Specific sensory stimuli*

   The trigger is sometimes a single specific sensory stimulus. A person who is auditory sensitive may become anxious when hearing a hand dryer or the hum of a data projector in the classroom, while someone who is visually sensitive may feel stressed in a room full of bright colours and flickering fluorescent lighting. People with tactile sensitivities are often observed rubbing their skin after someone has lightly brushed against them, as the input has been perceived as painful. They then become anxious in crowded environments or when standing in a queue, as they fear someone bumping into them. Others are anxious when expected to wear clothing or touch textures which they find uncomfortable. Table 4.2 provides examples of common sensory triggers for anxiety.

2. *Sensory overload*

   Others describe anxiety in response to multiple sensory stimuli. These individuals experience overload in 'sensory rich' environments. Places such as supermarkets, playparks, swimming pools, parties or busy streets bombard the senses with simultaneous stimuli at various intensities and frequencies. When this background stimuli is not filtered out, the individual becomes overwhelmed, triggering anxiety.

3. *Unpredictable sensory input*

   Another factor in sensory input which can contribute to anxiety for the autistic person is its unpredictability. Sources of noise, smell, visual input and touch are often sudden and fluctuate in volume, frequency and intensity. Most external input is beyond our control, and this in itself elicits fear and stress in individuals with autism.

   This fear of the unpredictable explains why people with autism often become anxious in new settings and activities. They do not know what sensory input awaits in new situations, so they try to control this by avoiding new experiences and withdrawing to familiar places and predictable routines.

4. *Sensory input in social interactions*

   Social interaction is another daily activity which carries considerable sensory input. People communicate using a constantly shifting array of facial expressions and gestures and vary the pitch and tone of their speech to add greater meaning. In addition to this, there may be tactile input involved in the interactions such as a hug or handshake. This can create sensory overload in social interactions and is a contributing factor in social withdrawal and isolation.

Point to remember

Some autistic people avoid eye contact because the visual input from facial expressions and body language can be overwhelming and confusing, leading to anxiety in interactions with others.

5. *Cumulative sensory input*

   Sensory stimulation is cumulative and so will build throughout the day, and individuals often reach a peak when they are so overwhelmed by input that they have an episode of high anxiety. Imagine that people start the day with an empty page, but, as they receive sensory input, the page begins to fill up until it becomes so crowded with input that there is no space for more. A hyperactive individual has a very small page, which fills up quickly, and when this happens, they often become extremely anxious and need time to calm down and 'clear the page'.

A common pattern is that the anxiety only becomes evident when the child/young person returns home from school. This may be because they have worked hard to tolerate the sensory input during the school day and to control their responses, but when they reach the 'safe environment' of home, they release the building anxiety.

These peak points of anxiety can of course happen at other times of the day also, and so it is important to observe and keep a record of such incidents to determine if there is a pattern, such as incidents always happening at the same time every day or a consistent trigger preceding the incident. When observing signs of anxiety to sensory stimuli, a broad range of behavioural responses may be seen.

Behavioural responses to sensory input

For some autistic people it may be difficult to identify and explain the nature of the sensory response. Some responses are impulsive and driven by an instinctive need for self-protection from input which is perceived as potentially harmful. As with other triggers for anxiety, sensory stimuli will elicit a fight, flight or freeze response and this may result in an unexpected response.

1. *Aggressive behaviours*

   Aggressive behaviours are often seen when the person has become highly anxious due to intense levels of sensory input. Sensory sensitivities can result in aggressive responses as the individual tries to stop the sensory input which is causing anxiety. In sensory terms, this may be described as 'sensory defensiveness', or can be seen as a 'fight' response as the individual tries to protect themself against input which is perceived as harmful.

Case example

Daniel, who is sensitive to tactile input, is standing in a queue. The person behind him accidentally nudges him, and Daniel responds by forcefully pushing him away.

Daniel experienced the unpredictable and light touch of the nudge as painful and so instinctively responded to protect himself against further harm.

An overstimulated person may damage objects which are causing noise, throw food due to the smell or taste of it, or hit out at people making too much noise or standing too close. These behaviours appear to be aggressive but are an instinctive mechanism of self-protection.

2. *Escape*

 Some individuals who feel overloaded by sensory input try to escape from the sensory source. In sensory terms, this may be defined as sensory avoidance, or it may be viewed as a 'flight' response. The individual may panic when faced with sensory input which they interpret as unpleasant or potentially dangerous, and try to run or hide.

 This can carry risk, as the anxiety caused by the sensory input will impact on the ability to think logically and analyse risk. They may therefore run across a busy car park or road when escaping from a shop, or may run out of school without permission.

 Some children or young people may engage in a negative behaviour as a means of escaping from an environment or activity which is causing heightened anxiety. They may have learnt that engaging in a behaviour such as screaming, damaging property or hurting a classmate will result in them being removed from the environment.

Case example

Emma is hyper-reactive to noise and touch, and so dislikes crowded environments. Every day in the school playground, she pushes or hits a classmate, and the consequence for this behaviour is 'time out' when she sits in a quiet part of the playground. Analysis of the behavioural pattern indicates that she is engaging in negative behaviours as she is feeling overwhelmed and anxious in the playground and it is her means of communicating that she wants to go to a quiet area.

3. *Shutdown*

 Some people are observed to become so overwhelmed by surrounding sensory input that they 'freeze' and the brain seems to almost shut down. The brain cannot select which input requires attention and which input should be blocked, and so it shuts out all input. The individual may appear unresponsive or sleepy and there may be physiological indictors such as nausea or change in pallor.

4. *Rigidity/insistence on sameness*

 Many people with autism become anxious when presented with a new activity or when expected to go a new place. They cannot predict what sensory input will be involved in the unfamiliar activity or setting and so may avoid novel experiences. Adherence to rigid routines and the preference for sameness which is associated with autism may be strategies to avoid new and unfamiliar sensory experiences.

Case example

Joseph is hyper-reactive to tactile input and so dislikes all forms of messy play. Every day during playtime in nursery he chooses to play with the jigsaws, followed by the train set and then builds with blocks. When the teacher tries to transition him to the water table, sand tray or painting easels, he becomes very upset and refuses to touch the materials. He immediately returns to one of his preferred activities.

5. *Repetitive behaviours*

   One of the core features of autism is repetitive behaviours, with common examples including flicking fingers in front of eyes, pacing, echolalia (repetitive vocalisations), tapping with hands or feet and rocking/swinging in a chair.

   When an individual with autism is in a heightened state of anxiety due to sensory hyper-reactivity, there is often an increase in repetitive behaviours. Many repetitive behaviours involve the individual seeking out increased levels of sensory input. This may seem paradoxical but these behaviours serve two functions. First, they block out unwanted sensory input as they enter the body and brain at a higher intensity than the sensory stimuli from the surrounding environment. Secondly, repetitive behaviours provide predictable input to individuals with autism and give a sense of control over the unfamiliar and unpredictable input around them.

Case example

Rebecca is observed flicking a piece of string close to her eyes and repeating a line from her favourite film. These behaviours increase in intensity and volume when she is anxious, specifically in the playground, the dining hall and when she goes to a new, unfamiliar place.

Rebecca's repetitive behaviours are helping her to block out confusing visual input as she focuses on the string instead, and blocks out loud and unpredictable noise by making her own loud, repetitive vocalisations.

Repetitive behaviours are often an indicator of anxiety in autism, and the behaviours are being used as a means of self-regulation as the input is predictable and familiar and therefore calming for the individual.

6. *Self-injury*

   Some children will engage in behaviours of an extremely high intensity in order to block out unwanted input and these can sometimes cause harm to themselves, for example a child who repeatedly bites their own hand. This biting causes pain and this then becomes the primary source of sensory stimulation and helps the child to block out overwhelming input from the surrounding environment. This type of behaviour is a clear indicator that the individual is experiencing very high levels of anxiety.

Conclusion

Individuals with autism frequently report that sensory sensitivities are one of the core contributing factors to their anxiety, and this is further supported by a growing body of research evidence. Sensory input can trigger fight, flight or freeze responses, and the sensory-based anxiety may cause increases in repetitive behaviours and a drive for sameness. Strategies which control the sensory environment and support the individual in achieving self-regulation of sensory input will be discussed in Chapter 6.

References

American Psychological Association (2013). *Diagnostic and Statistical Manual of Mental Disorders, 5th Edition: DSM-5.* Arlington, VA: American Psychiatric Association.

Ayres AJ (1989). *Sensory Integration and the Child, 25th Anniversary Edition.* Los Angeles, USA: Western Psychological Services.

Baum SH, Stevenson RA and Wallace MT (2015). Behavioral, perceptual, and neural alterations in sensory and multisensory function in autism spectrum disorder. *Progress in Neurobiology, 134,* 140–60.

Bitsika V, Mills R and Sharpley CF (2016). How are sensory features associated with seven anxiety disorders in boys with autism spectrum disorder? *International Journal of Developmental Neuroscience, 50,* 4–54.

Black KR, Stevenson RA, Segers M, Ncube BL, Sun SZ, Philipp-Muller A, Bebko JM, Barense MD and Ferber S (2017). Linking anxiety and insistence on sameness in autistic children: The role of sensory hypersensitivity. *Journal of Autism and Developmental Disorders, 47,* 2459–70.

Green SA, Ben-Sasson A, Soto TW and Carter AS (2012). Anxiety and sensory over-responsivity in toddlers with autism spectrum disorders: Bidirectional effects across time. *Journal of Autism and Developmental Disorders, 42,* 1112–9.

Harris A (2015). *Autism as a disABILITY.* Retrieved from TED www.youtube.com/watch?v=aPm4cK8FCVw

Lane SJ, Reynolds S and Dumenci L (2012). Sensory overresponsivity and anxiety in typically developing children and children with autism and attention deficit hyperactivity disorder: Cause or coexistence? *American Journal of Occupational Therapy, 66,* 595–603.

Neil L, Olsson NC and Pellicano E (2016). The relationship between intolerance of uncertainty, sensory sensitivities, and anxiety in autistic and typically developing children. *Journal of Autism and Developmental Disorders, 46,* 1962–73.

South M and Rodgers J (2017). Sensory, emotional and cognitive contributions to anxiety in autism spectrum disorders. *Frontiers in Human Neuroscience, 11,* 1–7.

Tomchek SD and Dunn W (2007). Sensory processing in children with and without autism: A comparative study using the short sensory profile. *American Journal of Occupational Therapy, 61,* 190–200.

Uljarevic M, Tennison O, Lane A, Kelly A and Leekam S (2016). Sensory subtypes and anxiety in older children and adolescents with autism spectrum disorder. *Autism Research, 9,* 1073–8.

Wigham s, Rodgers J, South M, McConachie H and Freeston M (2015). The interplay between sensory processing abnormalities, intolerance of uncertainty, anxiety and restricted and repetitive behaviours in autism spectrum disorder. *Journal of Autism and Developmental Disorders, 45,* 943–52.

5. Assessment of anxiety

Introduction

Assessment is an integral part of any education or intervention programme. It is important as it allows the child's educational and therapeutic team to identify and understand the child's unique set of strengths and difficulties.

Utilising a child's strengths within intervention approaches can make strategies more achievable and is likely to increase motivation and engagement in an intervention programme, especially when strategies may be more challenging. One of the main objectives of assessment is to identify areas of need or difficulty, which can then inform goal setting and intervention planning. When setting goals, it is important that both professionals and parents have identified focused areas in which skills need to be developed. Goals must be realistic and achievable, so often intervention begins with skills which are emerging rather than targeting areas of greatest difficulty.

Case example

Andrew was recently assessed by a psychologist due to an increase in repetitive behaviours and social withdrawal. Assessment indicated that he could not identify or label emotions, and therefore did not know to ask for help when anxious. Intervention goals focused on affective education to teach recognition of emotions so that he can communicate when he is feeling anxious. This is more realistic than expecting him to independently use a calming strategy at this stage.

Assessment can also be used to measure progress and evaluate the effectiveness of the intervention strategies. The child may be assessed before and after an anxiety management programme to determine if there has been a reduction in anxiety symptoms and behaviours, and if there has been improvement in the skills taught and a reduction in the experience of anxiety.

Identifying improvements is also important for children so they can celebrate their successes. Observing their own progress can foster a sense of achievement and develop confidence and self-esteem. This can increase motivation to continue with the intervention.

In some cases, assessment may show no change in anxiety symptoms or behaviour. Modifications or amendments to the intervention may be required to make it more appropriate to the individual, or professionals might need to consider an alternative set of strategies.

Point to remember

Assessment should identify strengths as well as difficulties. Strengths can then be incorporated into an intervention programme to assist skill development in other areas and to increase motivation.

Assessment methods can generally be separated into formal assessments and informal assessments.

Formal assessments

Formal assessments are generally used to compare an individual student's performance to that of his or her peers. Norm-referenced assessments are the most used standardised tests for formal assessment of a student. A standardised assessment has a set protocol which all testers must use, thus ensuring consistency.

A standardised assessment will contain the following:

- A specific set of test items which must be completed by everyone using the assessment.
- A clear set of instructions directing the examiner in how the assessment is to be administered to ensure consistency across examiners.
- A set of scoring instructions directing the user how to score each item.

Examples of norm-referenced assessments used for students with autism include:

- IQ – measuring cognitive and intellectual skills (this may include areas such as abstract thinking, problem solving and reasoning).
- Academic achievement – measuring academic skills across areas such as reading, writing and maths.
- Neuropsychological measures – these are more specialised assessment tools which assess specific features of neurocognitive functioning including memory, visual processing or executive functioning skills.

These standardised assessments will provide norm references for scoring. This means that the individual's score is compared to the scores obtained by a sample from the typical population. Scores from a sample will have been obtained during development of the assessment. This then allows the examiner to plot the individual's score as average or above/below average. Some assessments will also plot scores in terms of standard scores, percentile ranks and/or standard deviations.

Other formal assessments are criterion-referenced tests. These differ from norm-referenced assessments in that the purpose is to determine whether the individual student has achieved a specific skill or concept. This type of assessment scores the students' performance on the basis of whether or not the individual has performed each item correctly. In these assessments, there is usually an overall pass score. They differ from norm-referenced assessments in that they don't compare the students score to peer results. Criterion-referenced assessments are often used to assess specific areas of a student's communication or language ability and other adaptive life skills. Because criterion-referenced assessments identify precisely what a student can and cannot do they can be used to plan detailed and specific intervention which focuses on the individual student's difficulty.

Informal assessments

Informal assessments do not carry a set of standardised instructions or scores, and instead tend to be observation based. Notes may be made on the quality of the child or young person's performance in different tasks and then specific strengths and difficulties are highlighted. Oftentimes collecting informal data in the environment the child functions can be a better indicator of his or her ability (Smyth-Myles, 2010). As reported by Smyth-Myles, this type of information collected can be more valuable in comparison to data collected in a contrived formalised assessment environment. Informal observational assessment can be carried out by a range of people supporting the student with autism across several settings. Each person can observe and make notes on how the student behaves and performs when faced with different situations, activities and interactions. This method provides multiple sources of information, which builds a picture of how the child functions in school, home and community settings.

Point to remember

The formal assessment will give a clear set of scores, which can be useful in goal setting and measuring progress, while the informal assessment can add qualitative observation of skills which may be missed in the standardised assessments.

There are benefits and challenges associated with the use of both formal and informal assessments. If time permits, it is often useful to include both when assessing a child or young person.

Assessment of anxiety in autism

The presence of an anxiety disorder is not a core feature of autism but rather an independently co-occurring disorder that can be addressed. Assessing and identifying the type of anxiety and subsequently tailoring intervention to the autistic child can significantly improve quality of life.

Research consistently supports the prevalence of anxiety disorders in autism, but it has proven difficult to accurately measure and differentiate anxiety symptoms and autism. This difficulty arises from the similarity in some of the features of anxiety and autism. Social avoidance, communication difficulties and the presence of repetitive and restrictive behaviours are common to both autism and anxiety (Cath et al., 2008). The causes for these challenges, however, will be different. Social avoidance in typical anxiety, for example, is usually a fear of negative evaluation from others (social anxiety), whereas social avoidance in autism may be due to disinterest in interaction with others. Many autistic children cannot report their internal experiences and fears; however, professionals commonly rely on self-report when assessing similar behaviour symptoms (Kerns et al., 2016).

Kerns et al. (2014) found that individuals with autism present with both typical anxiety symptoms and atypical anxiety symptoms. Atypical anxiety symptoms included unusual phobias, excessive worry about change, the presence of ritualistic behaviour not attributable to intrusive unwanted thoughts as seen in obsessive-compulsive disorder, and social fear not related to negative judgement by others (Ozsivadjian et al., 2012; Trembath et al., 2012). The presence of atypical anxiety characteristics alongside the overlap of autism and anxiety symptoms has led researchers to query whether anxiety measures used with typically developing children can be effectively used to measure anxiety in autistic children.

All assessment tools which are used for measuring anxiety in children can be used with autistic individuals, but most have not been adapted for the specific needs of an autistic child. Rodgers et al. (2016) have developed an adapted version of the Revised Children's Anxiety and Depression Scale (RCADS) for children with autism known as the Anxiety Scale for Children – ASD (ASC-ASD).

Assessments which involve clinical interview or structured interview schedule include:

- Anxiety Disorders Interview Schedule-Child (ADIS-C) (Silverman and Albano, 2004)
- Child and Adolescent Symptom Inventory (CASI -4) (Gadow and Sprafkin, 2005)
- Paediatric Anxiety Rating Scale (PARS) (Research Units of Pediatric Psychopharmacology, Riddle and Greenhill, 2002)

Other measurement tools involve self-report, such as:

- Beck Youth Inventories Second Edition for Children and Adolescents (BYI-II) (Beck and Beck, 2005)
- Spence Children's Anxiety Scale (SCAS) (Spence, 1998)
- Multidimensional Anxiety Scale for Children, 2nd edition (MASC-2) (March, 2012)
- Screen for Child Anxiety Related Emotional Disorders (SCARED) (Birmaher et al., 1995)
- RCADS (Chorpita et al., 2015)

Some of these can be completed by a parent or teacher for children who have difficulties with self-reporting. Self-reporting is frequently used to assess anxiety in typically developing children, whereas for children with autism assessment has centred on parental report (Grondhuis and Aman, 2012; Lecavalier et al., 2014). Self-report has been used less frequently with autistic children as intellectual difficulties and/or poorer social cognition skills may impact their ability to accurately report on their own symptom (Dyck et al., 2001; Ozsivadjian et al., 2012).

Research into the efficacy of self-report is limited. Several studies show that children can report on their own behaviours and symptoms. However, they found that children tend to report fewer autistic traits or greater social competency skills compared to their parents (Pearl et al., 2016). A study by Knott and colleagues reports a positive correlation between child and parents scores, although the parental scores indicated greater symptom severity, frequency and rate in comparison to the child's self-report of symptoms (Knott et al., 2006). This suggests that self-report can form part of a comprehensive assessment approach. However, there are limitations to using self-report measures on their own.

When administering assessment tools including self-report measures it is important to consider modifications which can be made to meet the needs of the student. Prior to beginning assessment spend some time engaging in a preferred activity with the student, possibly related to their special interest, to build rapport and reduce anxiety. Use a visual schedule to indicate to the student how many activities they need to complete and refer to this throughout the assessment so they have a clear understanding of how many are left before completion. Take care to limit sensory distractions in the environment: consideration should be given to the student's sensory preferences including seating, use of fidget items and short breaks.

Various research studies have reviewed the appropriateness of assessment tools in autism. Lecavalier et al. (2014) reviewed ten anxiety measures for use in autism clinical trials, and this study found that the ADIS-C, MASC, CASI-4R and PARS were appropriate to be utilised with pupils with autism with conditions. In addition the SCARED, RCADS and the Anxiety, Depression and Mood Scale (ADAMS) (Esbensen et al., 2003) were identified as potentially appropriate. Other studies have explored the reliability and validity of these anxiety measures. Storch et al. (2012) reported PARS to demonstrate acceptable validity and reliability when used with autistic young people seeking intervention for anxiety. However, internal consistency and parent–child agreement were limited. Parent–child agreement on the Anxiety Disorders Interview Schedule for DSM-IV: Child and Parent Version (ADIS-C/P) was also found to be poor in one study, which highlights the importance of also attaining parent report rather than relying on child report alone (Ung et al., 2014). White and colleagues (2012) also found poor parent and child agreement when using the CASI-4.

A study by Wigham and McConachie (2014) reviewed eight assessment tools used with autistic children. Their results indicated that the SCAS, RCADS and SCARED are considered to be robust tools in terms of measurement properties.

Assessment measures

ADIS-C (Silverman and Albano, 2004) – This is a semi-structured interview used to assess anxiety disorders in children aged 7–17. This tool has shown inter-rater reliability in children and young people with autism. However, one study found poor parent–child agreement (Storch et al., 2012).

ADIS-ASA (Kerns et al., 2017) – Kerns and colleagues further developed the ADIS-C to include an autism addendum, and this measure aims to differentiate between traditional anxiety symptoms from symptoms of autism. Results from their study provide evidence for reliability and validity of the ADIS-ASA as a measure for traditional type symptoms and partial support for its validity in measuring ambiguous anxiety-like symptoms (Kerns et al., 2017). This measure has demonstrated its ability to differentiate overlapping anxiety-like behaviours in autism such as fear of change, fears related to social interaction, and sensory and special interest fears from co-occurring anxiety disorders.

RCADS (Chorpita et al., 2015) – this is a 47-item measure of anxiety and depression with six subscales: panic, separation anxiety, obsessive–compulsive behaviour, generalised, social anxiety and depression. It has good psychometric properties for typically developing children and is considered a robust measure for use in autism (Wigham and McConachie, 2014).

ASD-ASC (Rodgers et al., 2016) – this scale is a modified version of RCADS with the addition of four anxiety subscales in both the child and parent scales: performance anxiety, uncertainty, anxious arousal and separation anxiety. Initial evaluation of the scale demonstrates good validity, reliability and internal consistency (Rodgers et al., 2016).

PARS (Research Units of Pediatric Psychopharmacology, Riddle and Greenhill, 2002) – this is a clinician-rated scale for children and young people aged 7–17 years based on a joint parent and child interview. PARS assesses somatic, separation specific, social and generalised symptoms of anxiety disorders. As highlighted, PARS shows good reliability and validity for use with individuals with autism.

SCAS (Spence, 1998) – this is a 44-item scale for children aged 7 to 14 years. It measures symptoms of separation anxiety, social anxiety, obsessive–compulsive disorder, panic, generalised anxiety and physical injury fears. It shows acceptable internal consistency and parent–child agreement within autism sample, although internal consistency is not strong for all subscales (Ozsivadjian et al., 2014).

CASI-4 (Gadow and Sprafkin, 1998) – this is a 120–163-item parent scale which assesses symptoms for various DSM-IV disorders including 26 anxiety items related to symptoms of social, separation, and generalised anxiety, post-traumatic stress and obsessive–compulsive disorder. Sukhodolsky developed a reduced 20-item scale which shows good internal consistency in children with autism (Sukhodolsky et al., 2008).

MASC (March, 2012) – this is a parent and child report measure of anxiety within four domains: physical symptoms, social anxiety, harm avoidance and separation/panic. This scale shows good internal validity (Wood et al., 2009); however, it is dependent on language ability and further validation of use in autism is required.

SCARED (Birmaher et al., 1995) – this is a 41-item child and parent report measure for pupils aged 4–18 that assesses symptoms related to separation, social and generalised anxiety disorders. It has demonstrated sensitivity and specificity for anxiety disorders and consistency between child and parent reports in a small sample. However, this was limited (Kerns et al., 2015) and showed moderate convergent reliability (Stern et al., 2014).

There is not yet a gold standard assessment tool for measuring anxiety in autistic children. The ADIS-ASA and ASD-ASC are measurement tools designed to investigate more varied symptoms of anxiety in autism. The measures identified above may support assessment of anxiety in autism when used as part of a transdiagnostic approach. However, they should be used with caution when assessing anxiety for pupils who are not currently seeking treatment (Kerns et al., 2015).

For optimal assessment it is advised that assessment is triangulated where possible using parent, teacher (or other) and self-report (where appropriate). Assessment may also include behavioural scales and measures of cognitive ability to obtain a baseline measure of functional ability. Examples of such assessment include the Adapative Behaviour Assessment System (Oakland and

Harrison, 2015), Vineland Adaptive Behaviour Scales (Sparrow et al., 2016) or Wechsler Individual Achievement Test (Wechsler, 2017). Other areas of assessment related to anxiety in autism include:

- Intolerance of uncertainty – Intolerance of Uncertainty Scale (Buhr and Dugas, 2002)
- Cognitive flexibility – Behaviour Rating Inventory of Executive Function (Gioia et al., 2000)
- Alexithymia – Toronto Alexithymia Scale-20 (TAS-20) (Bagby et al., 1994); Childrens Alexithymia Scale (Rieffe et al., 2006)
- Emotional regulation – Emotional Dysregulation Inventory (Mazefsky et al., 2018)

Conclusion

There are many types of assessment tools available including structured, semi-structured assessments, observational and parent and/or self-report measures. Accurate assessment of anxiety can be challenging due to symptom overlap with co-existing disorders, limitations of self-report and a lack of validated measurement tools which are sensitive to the atypical presentation of anxiety in autism (Vasa and Mazurek, 2015). In addition, there are challenges associated with formal assessment environments; oftentimes children, including those with autism, may be more or less likely to display particular behaviours within structured assessment compared to when engaged in free-play.

Therefore, a comprehensive assessment approach is required with the administration of multiple assessment tools and gathering information from multiple sources alongside observation within multiple settings across time. In some cases, a comprehensive profile of the child's challenges, needs and strengths can be evaluated through a combination of observations across settings, alongside informal reports from those working and living with the individual. It is important to include self-report methods as appropriate, ensuring the individual is given suitable supports to communicate effectively. It is important to note that many of the formal anxiety assessments tools should be used with caution as they may not measure the factors specific to autism.

References

Bagby RM, Parker JDA and Taylor GJ (1994). The twenty-item Toronto Alexithymia Scale-I. Item selection and cross-validation of the factor structure. *Journal of Psychosomatic Research*, *38*, 23–32.

Beck AT and Beck JS (2005). *Beck Youth Inventories Second Edition for Children and Adolescents*. New York: Pearson Education.

Birmaher B, Khetarpal S, Cully M, Brent D and McKenzie S (1995). *Screen for Child Anxiety Related Emotional Disorders*. Pittsburgh: Western Psychiatric Institute & Clinic, Department of Child Psychology.

Buhr K and Dugas MJ (2002). The intolerance of uncertainty scale: psychometric properties of the English version. *Behaviour Research and Therapy*, *40*, 931–945.

Cath DC, Ran N, Smit JH, van Balkom AJ and Comijs HC (2008). Symptom overlap between autism spectrum disorder, generalized social anxiety disorder and obsessive-compulsive disorder in adults: a preliminary case-controlled study. *Psychopathology*, *41*, 101–110.

Chorpita BF, Ebesutani C and Spence SH (2015). *Revised Children's Anxiety and Depression Scale*. Los Angeles: Child First.

Dyck MJ, Ferguson K and Shochet IM (2001). Do autism spectrum disorders differ from each other and from non-spectrum disorders on emotion recognition tests? *European Child and Adolescent Psychiatry*, *10*, 105–116.

Esbensen AJ, Rojahn J, Aman MG and Ruedrich S (2003). Reliability and validity of an assessment instrument for anxiety, depression, and mood among individuals with mental retardation. *Journal of Autism and Developmental Disorders*, *33*, 617–629.

Gadow KD and Sprafkin J (1998). *Adolescent symptom inventory-4 norms manual*. Stony Brook, NY: Checkmate Plus.

Gadow KD and Sprafkin J (2005). *Child and Adolescent Symptom Inventory-4 Revised (CASI-4R)*. Stony Brook: Checkmate Plus.

Gioia G, Isquith P, Guy S and Kenworthy L (2000). *Behavior Rating Inventory of Executive Function*. Odessa, FL, USA: Psychological Assessment Resources.

Grondhuis SN and Aman MG (2012). Assessment of anxiety in children and adolescents with autism spectrum disorders. *Research in Autism Spectrum Disorders*, *6*, 1345–1365.

Kerns CM, Kendall PC, Berry L, Souders MC, Franklin ME, Schultz RT, Miller J and Herrington J (2014). Traditional and atypical presentations of anxiety in youth with autism spectrum disorder. *Journal of Autism and Developmental Disorders*, *44*, 2851–2861.

Kerns CM, Maddox BB, Kendall PC, Rump K, Berry L, Schultz RT, Souders MC, Bennett A, Herrington J and Miller J (2015). Brief measures of anxiety in non-treatment-seeking youth with autism spectrum disorder. *Autism*, *19*, 969–979.

Kerns CM, Renno P, Kendall PC, Wood JJ and Storch EA (2017). Anxiety disorders interview schedule-autism addendum: reliability and validity in children with autism spectrum disorder. *Journal of Clinical Child and Adolescent Psychology*, *46*, 88–100.

Kerns CM, Rump K, Worley J, Kratz H, McVey A, Herrington J and Miller J (2016). The differential diagnosis of anxiety disorders in cognitively-able youth with autism. *Cognitive and Behavioral Practice*, *23*(4), 530–547.

Knott F, Dunlop AW and Mackay T (2006). Living with ASD: how do children and their parents assess their difficulties with social interaction and understanding? *Autism*, *10*(6), 609–617.

Lecavalier L, Wood JJ, Halladay AK, Jones NE, Aman MG, Cook EH, Handen BL, King BH, Pearson DA, Hallett V and Sullivan KA (2014). Measuring anxiety as a treatment endpoint in youth with autism spectrum disorder. *Journal of Autism and Developmental Disorders*, *44*, 1128–1143.

March JS (2012). *Multidimensional Anxiety Scale for Children, 2nd Edition*. Toronto, USA: Multi-Health Systems Inc.

Mazefsky CA, Day TN, Siegel M, White SW, Yu L and Pilkonis PA (2018). Development of the emotion dysregulation inventory: A PROMIS®ing method for creating sensitive and unbiased questionnaires for autism spectrum disorder. *Journal of Autism and Developmental Disorders*, *48*, 3736–3746.

Oakland and Harrison (2015). *Adaptive Behavior Assessment System (ABAS-3) - Third Edition*. London: Pearson.

Ozsivadjian A, Hibberd C and Hollocks MJ (2014). Brief report: the use of self-report measures in young people with autism spectrum disorder to access symptoms of anxiety, depression and negative thoughts. *Journal of Autism and Developmental Disorders*, *44*, 969–974.

Ozsivadjian A, Knott F and Magiati I (2012). Parent and child perspectives on the nature of anxiety in children and young people with autism spectrum disorders: a focus group study. *Autism*, *16*, 107–121.

Pearl A, Edwards EM and Murray MJ (2016). Comparison of self-and other-report of symptoms of autism and co-morbid psychopathology in adults with autism spectrum disorder. *Contemporary Behavioral Health Care*. 2, 1–8.

Research Units of Pediatric Psychopharmacology, Riddle MA and Greenhill LL (2002). Paediatric Anxiety Rating Scale: (PARS): Development and psychometric properties. *Journal of the American Academy of Child and Adolescent Psychiatry*, *41*, 1061–1069.

Rieffe C, Oosterveld P and Terwogt MM (2006). An alexithymia questionnaire for children: factorial and concurrent validation results. *Personality and Individual Differences*, *40*, 123–133.

Rodgers J, Wigham S, McConachie H, Freeston M, Honey E and Parr JR (2016). Development of the anxiety scale for children with autism spectrum disorder (ASC-ASD). *Autism Research*, *9*, 1205–1215.

Silverman WK and Albano AM (2004). *Anxiety Disorders Interview Schedule-Child.* Albany, NY: Graywind Publications.

Smyth-Myles B (2010) Research Bulletin '*Enabling Education*', Middletown Centre for Autism. www.middletownautism.com/files/uploads/e172e242d989810728e2b9dd26b2ef90.pdf Last Accessed 27th November 2019.

Sparrow SS, Cicchetti DV and Saulnier CA (2016). *Vineland Adaptive Behavior Scales, Third Edition (Vineland-3).* London: Pearson.

Spence SH (1998). *Spence Children's Anxiety Scale.* www.scaswebsite.com/

Stern JA, Gadgil MS, Blakeley-Smith A, Reaven JA and Hepburn SL (2014). Psychometric properties of the SCARED in youth with autism spectrum disorder. *Research in Autism Spectrum Disorders*, *8*, 1225–1234.

Storch EA, Wood JJ, Ehrenreich-May J, Jones AM, Park JM, Lewin AB and Murphy TK (2012). Convergent and discriminant validity and reliability of the pediatric anxiety rating scale in youth with autism spectrum disorders. *Journal of Autism and Developmental Disorders*, *42*, 2374–2382.

Sukhodolsky DG, Scahill L, Gadow KD, Arnold LE, Aman MG, McDougle CJ, McCracken JT, Tierney E, White SW, Lecavalier L and Vitiello B (2008). Parent-rated anxiety symptoms in children with pervasive developmental disorders: frequency and association with core autism symptoms and cognitive functioning. *Journal of Abnormal Child Psychology*, *36*(1), 117–128.

Trembath D, Germano C, Johanson G and Dissanayake C (2012). The experience of anxiety in young adults with autism spectrum disorders. *Focus on Autism and Other Developmental Disabilities*, *27*, 213–224.

Ung D, Arnold EB, De Nadai AS, Lewin AB, Phares V, Murphy TK and Storch EA (2014). Inter-rater reliability of the anxiety disorders interview schedule for DSM-IV in high-functioning youth with autism spectrum disorder. *Journal of Developmental and Physical Disabilities*, *26*, 53–65.

Vasa RA and Mazurek MO (2015). An update on anxiety in youth with autism spectrum disorders. *Current Opinion in Psychiatry*, *28*(2), 83.

Wechsler D (2017). *Wechsler Individual Achievement Test - Third UK Edition (WIAT-III UK).* London: Pearson.

White SW, Schry AR and Maddox BB (2012). Brief report: the assessment of anxiety in high-functioning adolescents with autism spectrum disorder. *Journal of Autism and Developmental Disorders*, *42*, 1138–1145.

Wigham S. and McConachie H (2014). Systematic review of the properties of tools used to measure outcomes in anxiety intervention studies for children with autism spectrum disorders. *PLoS ONE*, *9*(1). *Article e85268.*

Wood JJ, Drahota A, Sze K, Van Dyke M, Decker K, Fujii C, Bahng C, Renno P, Hwang W-C and Spiker M (2009). Brief report: effects of cognitive behavioral therapy on parent-reported autism symptoms in school-age children with high-functioning autism. *Journal of Autism and Developmental Disorders*, *39*, 1608.

6. Anxiety management strategies for autistic children and young people

Introduction

This chapter will provide information on effective interventions for anxiety management in autism. A dual approach is often taken to anxiety intervention:

- Reducing or removing triggers where possible
- Supporting the individual in developing strategies to better cope with potential triggers

Anxiety management programmes usually integrate both proactive and reactive strategies. Proactive strategies are designed to reduce the risk of anxiety occurring or escalating; they include strategies to equip the child with appropriate communication, emotional regulation and life skills. Reactive strategies are designed to keep the child and those around them safe from harm should they become anxious and/or distressed.

Point to remember

Following assessment, the individual's potential triggers for anxiety should be identified and a proactive management plan developed. It is better to prevent escalating anxiety than to wait for the first indicators of stress or worry.

A good anxiety plan should have more proactive than reactive strategies. An individualised approach to anxiety management should be considered drawing on more than one approach to suit the needs of each individual child. Any anxiety plan should contain a range of individualised strategies that have, where possible, been developed in partnership with the child or young person. These strategies should evolve as the person develops and experiences new milestones and challenges.

This chapter provides suggestions for strategies to address anxiety and is divided into two parts:

Section One: simple strategies, structured teaching, Social Stories™ and comic strip conversations, environmental strategies, sensory strategies, desensitisation, the stress kit, relaxation exercises and mindfulness.

Section Two: cognitively-based approaches, cognitive behavioural style strategies, thinking tools, coping cards, self-regulation, affective education, The Incredible 5 Point Scale, co-regulation.

Section one

Simple Strategies that can be used alongside all other strategies:

Removal of the trigger

The first thing we may be able to do is to remove or reduce the trigger if possible. Once we do this, we should follow-up by engaging the individual in some gentle relaxation strategies to soothe their anxiety response.

It is important to note that if we only try to remove triggers in situations, we can inhibit child development and experiences needed to build resilience. Therefore, we may start by removing the trigger, but also work towards building a tolerance. For example, increasing a child's tolerance of the school bell could begin with allowing the child to wear earphones and then gradually exposing them to the noise in a controlled manner.

For us to best facilitate a child or young person understanding their triggers, we must take time to observe them closely across environments/situations; this is key to effectively supporting them. We must identify trigger situations in school – for example, transitioning from one class to another, break and lunchtimes, group work which leads to anxiety. Observing how the individual manages during unstructured time, for example break and lunch times, is also informative. Many children and young adults will have difficulty knowing intuitively how to fill this unstructured social time, leaving them feeling alone and anxious, as they struggle to participate in typical social chit chat. Using visual timetables, Social Stories™, lunchtime clubs or other visual aids (e.g. choice boards) to address social communication issues and help increase predictability, may prove beneficial. For younger children, placing emphasis on sensory play, and employing the expertise of an occupational therapist to address any sensory differences with their coordination/motor abilities, may help during their structured play activities.

Point to remember

In the sort-term, triggers may be reduced or removed in order to de-escalate anxiety and improve engagement in activity. In the long-term, the aim is to gradually desensitise the child to the trigger and improve coping skills.

Flexibility

Be flexible with your expectations.

A child's anxiety may fluctuate from day to day and throughout the day. It is not always possible to predict emotional states or to control triggers, so supporting adults need to adopt a sensitive and flexible approach. The individual may be able to cope with a high level of demands on some days, but when anxious, the ability to cope with demands decreases.

When the child is showing signs of anxiety, demands at home and school should be reduced to a level appropriate to their emotional state. This will avoid an exacerbation of the anxiety. In school, this may involve reducing the number of assigned tasks and providing more calm breaks. At home, this may involve cancelling social plans and removing expectations for household chores.

Communication

How does the child respond to communication? How does the child communicate their needs?

Verbal instructions and interactions can be a trigger for anxiety due to difficulties in processing and retaining verbal information. The risk of creating or escalating anxiety can be reduced by following some simple communication strategies when interacting with an autistic child:

1. Use visual supports to replace or augment verbal language.
2. Ensure the visual supports are appropriate for the child's communicative level. If they cannot understand the visual support, this will further increase anxiety. The individual may require the use of objects, photographs, symbols or written words to support communication.
3. Keep visual supports accessible. Visuals both support verbal instructions and aid expressive communication.
4. Keep verbal instructions and prompts short and simple.
5. Allow processing time. This will vary for each child, but it can take several seconds, or sometimes minutes, for an individual with autism to process, understand and respond to a verbal instruction or question.

Point to remember

Introduce visual supports when the child is calm; do not use for the first time when the child is anxious. Teach in a one-to-one setting initially and provide opportunity for practice.

Formalised approaches

These approaches are usable at home but also provide opportunities for formal training packages to increase skills.

Structured teaching

A structured environment should be easily understandable and predictable, and the child should understand what is happening. The expectations of the task or activity should be immediately clear. This approach supports acquisition of new skills and generalisation of these skills from one setting to another.

The University of North Carolina formalises structured teaching in the TEACCH approach. TEACCH approach focuses on four key components of visual structure:

1. Physical environment
2. Visual schedules
3. Activity systems
4. Structured tasks

1. Physical environment

A structured environment reduces anxiety by providing clear visual cues of what is expected in the environment, therefore removing the need for complex verbal instructions of where to go and what to do in different contexts. Another important aim of physical structure is to reduce sensory stimulation. Screens (or similar) of varying heights are often used to reduce visual distractions, which then reduces the risk of becoming overwhelmed by surrounding stimuli.

2. Visual schedules

Visual schedules provide predictability by setting out a planned routine in a format which is easily understood by the autistic child. It removes the need for complex verbal explanations and is readily available, so can be checked as often as required.

Schedules are individualised to ensure they are presented in a way that is meaningful to the person using the schedule. Some schedules may only show 1–2 activities at a time, while others may present a part-day or full-day schedule, dependent on how much information the individual can process.

The type of visual supports used on schedules can include objects, photographs, symbols or words, again depending on what the child can understand independently. The ability to process and understand information can deteriorate when the person is anxious, and so it is important to ensure that the type of visual support used is meaningful to the individual even when in a high state of anxiety.

Schedules can also manage anxiety by preparing the child for changes to the daily routine. A visual support to indicate a change to planned activities can be inserted to the schedule to clarify when an activity has been cancelled or delayed and what will happen instead.

3. Activity systems

Activity (or work) systems are used when the child is engaged in an activity which involves multiple parts, for example completing a series of homework tasks or carrying out a sequence of personal care tasks in the morning.

The activity system clarifies what is to be done, how many parts are involved, in what order the parts should be completed and how the child knows when they are finished. Activity systems help to reduce anxiety as they visually clarify what is expected without the need for ongoing verbal prompting. Figure 6.1 is an example of an activity system for showering and Figure 6.2 provides an example of a personal care activity system.

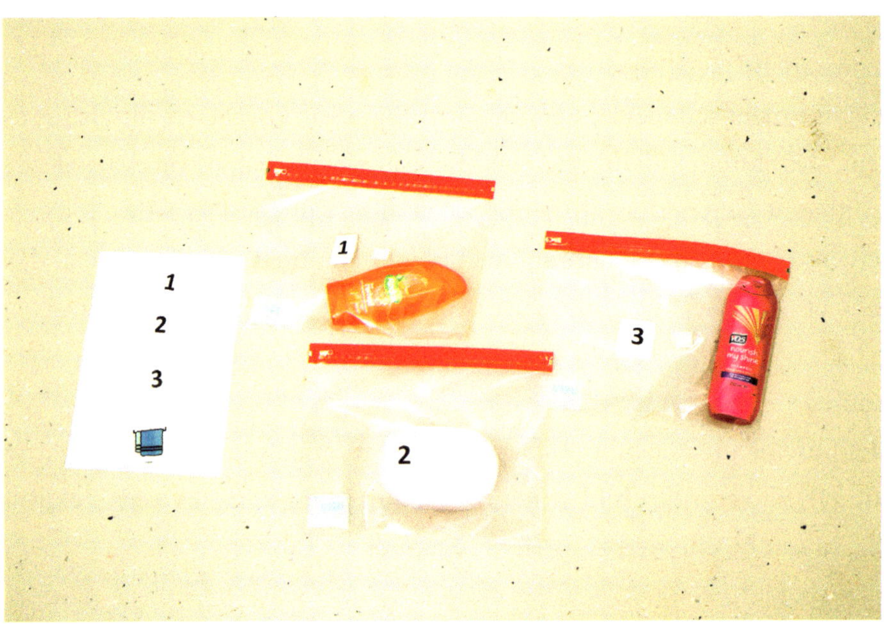

Figure 6.1 Showering activity system

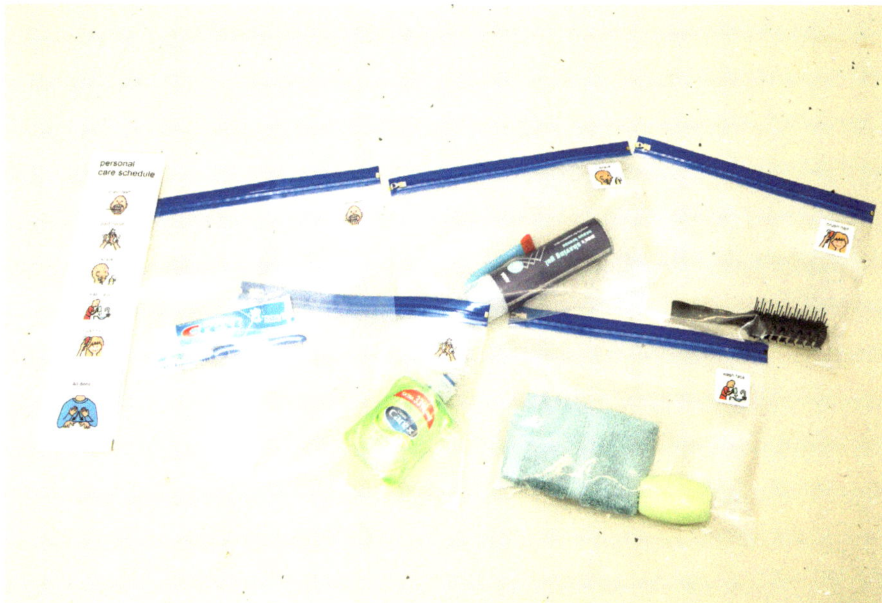

Figure 6.2 Personal care activity system

4. Structured tasks

Tasks presented to a child should contain some level of visual structure. Examples of visual structure include setting out materials in the order in which they are to be used for an activity or providing step-by-step written instructions for a task. The visual structure instructs and clarifies so the individual understands what is to be done without the need for complex verbal instructions. This reduces anxiety as the student can refer back to the visual supports during the task instead of retaining verbal instructions. Figure 6.3 is an example of how to structure a construction type play activity. Figure 6.4 also illustrates how to structure a task, using the example of brushing teeth.

Figure 6.3 Structured task for play

Figure 6.4 Structured task for brushing teeth

For further information on the TEACCH approach visit https://teacch.com/

Story-based interventions and social communication

Social Stories™

Social Stories™, developed by Carol Gray, are used to support autistic children in developing social understanding. They are often used to prevent or reduce anxiety in social situations. A social story includes a short description of a social event or activity and detailed, specific information to the reader about what to expect in that situation and why. The skills required in specific situations may need to be explicitly taught.

Carol Gray provides a full history on the development and use of Social Stories™ on her website https://carolgraysocialstories.com/social-stories/

> A social story accurately describes a context, skill, achievement or concept according to 10 defining criteria. These criteria guide Story research, development, and implementation to ensure an overall patient and supportive quality, and a format, 'voice', content, and learning experience that is descriptive, meaningful, and physically, socially, and emotionally safe for the child, adolescent, or adult with autism.
>
> (Gray, 2018)

Research conducted by Reynhout and Carter (2009) found Social Stories™ to be an acceptable and effective intervention. This research study interviewed teachers and sought their opinion on the acceptability, applicability and efficacy of Social Stories™. Findings from research suggest Social Stories™ are appropriate for a wide variety of children, behaviours and abilities and can be implemented in a wide variety of settings and that are complementary to other interventions (Crozier & Tincani, 2007; Delano & Snell, 2006; Scattone et al., 2006).

Social Stories™ are written in the first person and may contain photographs and/or symbols. They should be read frequently before the event and the child or young person can bring the social story to the situation to serve as a visual prompt. This provides planning and consistency, which can ease anxiety about upcoming events.

Social Stories™ can be used to describe and explain distressing experiences or events, for example nightmares, moving to a new house or changes in family circumstances. They can be used as a behavioural strategy to support understanding and development of adaptive skills, for example what to do when angry or anxious. Social Stories™ are also used to develop and teach other skills such as self-care skills. Some Social Stories™ are used to provide positive feedback by describing and celebrating achievements or area of strength.

Comic strip conversations

Comic strip conversations (also developed by Carol Gray) are another tool used to provide clarity in social situations to reduce anxiety. They use visual representations of social interactions by using symbols, line drawings and colour. Comic strip conversations can successfully depict abstract aspects of social communication in concrete drawings, which makes it easier for the autistic student to understand (Gray, 1994).

Point to remember

A comic strip conversation should not be used when the child is still anxious or recovering from a challenging situation. It should be introduced when the child is calm enough to process information and be an active contributor to the process.

Comic strip conversations use a mixture of thought and speech bubbles to outline the feelings and intentions of others. They are also a useful tool to gain insight into the perspective of the child in social situations. The process can support the person in identifying possible solutions or strategies for future social situations and allows the supporting adult to give direction on how to approach situations differently. This helps to raise awareness of social skills which could be used to reduce confusion and anxiety in future social scenarios.

Green: Good ideas, happy, friendly
Red: Bad ideas, angers, unfriendly
Blue: Sad, uncomfortable
Yellow: Frightened
Black: Facts, truth
Orange: Questions
Brown: Comfortable, cosy
Purple: Proud
Colour combinations: Confusion

Figure 6.5 Example of colour coding feelings and intentions

When using comic strip conversations, the child takes a lead role with the supporting adult offering guidance. The aim is to identify what others say and do and to build awareness of what other people, their peers, siblings and teachers may be thinking. For this reason, the supporting adult may ask questions about the situation or social interaction. Examples of questions include:

- Where are you?
- Who is there?
- What are you doing?
- What did you say?
- What did others say?
- What did you think when you said that?
- What did others think when they said/did that?

Colour can be used to define the feelings and intentions of the characters within the illustration as shown in Figure 6.5.

It is essential to ensure the child can read and use a pen/pencil before commencing the use of comic strip conversations. They also need to be able to understand and discriminate between visual symbols. Carol Gray (1994) provides a symbol dictionary to aid this teaching process. To introduce the concept and pre-teach the skills required it is useful to begin with a comic strip conversation based on a situation which is familiar to the child. This allows the gradual introduction of the various symbols to be used and builds confidence in the child's ability to engage in the intervention.

Environmental and sensory strategies

Creating a low arousal environment

The creation of a low arousal environment is a key proactive strategy in anxiety management. This is achieved through the minimisation of sensory input, reducing the intensity of stimuli and controlling the amount of unpredictable information. It is useful to carry out an audit or checklist of the setting and consider how sensory stimulation could be best managed to create a calm environment.

Some key principles in creating a low arousal environment are listed in Table 6.1.

Table 6.1 Creating a low arousal environment

Input	Example of adaptations
Visual	• Use of muted, pastel colours on walls and floors. • Reduce visual display boards in classrooms. • Avoid patterned wallpaper, carpet, curtains etc. • Use dimmed lighting. • Turn off TVs, computers etc, when not in use. • Provision of an area with reduced visual input where work can be completed. • Provision of sunglasses.
Auditory	• Use soft furnishings (e.g. mats, cushions) to absorb noises. • Put rubber feet on chairs and tables. • Removal of school bells. • Control noise levels in the classroom using a visual support, e.g. a volume control symbol. • Use of ear defenders (see section on desensitisation). • Control volume and amount of verbal interaction.
Tactile (touch)	• Allow pupil to stand at the back of the lines and end of rows as a means of providing more personal space. • Place visual markers on the floor to show where each pupil should stand to prevent close physical proximity of others. • Allow pupil to leave class five minutes early to avoid busy corridors. • Provide non-contact sports and activities in PE and the playground. • Provide alternative materials in Art (e.g. pencils and computer work instead of paint and clay). • Limit time the child is expected to engage in 'messy play' activities. • Visit shops, swimming pools, cinemas etc at quieter times to avoid crowds. • Flexibility in school uniform policy, e.g. permitting polo shirt instead of shirt and tie. • Remove labels from clothing. • Provision of seamless socks. • Provide wipes or hand sanitiser instead of washing hands under running water. • Allow the child to wash at sink or have a bath instead of using a shower.
Olfactory (smell)	• Keep rooms well ventilated, e.g. windows open when cooking; windows open in bathroom. • Use of odourless soaps, shower gels, deodorants etc. • Provision of a favourite smell on a piece of cloth which the child can then hold up to nose to block out unwanted smells. • Adults may need to avoid wearing perfumes or strongly scented sprays. • Avoid use of air fresheners in rooms.
Gustatory (taste)	• Provision of preferred food items at mealtimes. • Do not coerce a child to eat non-preferred food items.

(*Continued*)

Table 6.1 (Cont.)

Input	Example of adaptations
Vestibular (movement)	• Provide activities which do not involve backward or spinning movements, i.e. avoid swings, roundabouts etc. • Ensure toilets and chairs are at appropriate height, i.e. individual's feet should be firmly on the floor when seated. • If chair or toilet is too high, provide a box or step on which feet are placed when seated. • If the child dislikes being off the floor, consider appropriate equipment in PE, i.e. avoid wall bars, ropes, balance beams. Activities should instead be completed at floor level.
Proprioception	• Prepare the child for movement. • Avoid sudden, unpredictable movements.
Interoception	• Ensure the child has a way of communicating needs, e.g. hunger, thirst, toilet. • If individual is unable to recognise or communicate these needs, the supporting adult should be observant of the needs and respond accordingly. • Ensure environments are not too warm or too cold.

Calm breaks

Calm breaks are a proactive strategy, ensuring the child stays regulated throughout the day. They are incorporated as part of the daily routine, even on days when anxiety levels seem low. **Calm breaks are not a reward and should not be contingent on behaviour**. The child will be even more dependent on calm breaks on a challenging day. The break should be provided before the child is in a heightened state of anxiety. Pre-empting a rise in anxiety or stress will assist the child to cope more effectively with challenges as they will be in a calmer state when approaching activities.

When planning calm breaks the following factors should be considered:

1. Location of calm break

   In school, calm breaks may take place in:
   - A quiet room with minimal stimulation
   - A calm room equipped with sensory resources
   - A pop-up tent
   - A corner of the classroom screened off with minimal sensory stimulation
   - Older students may use quiet spaces in school, such as the locker room (when other students are in class) or an empty office or classroom.

   At home, calm breaks may take place in:
   - Own bedroom if it is associated with a place of calmness
   - A pop-up tent

- An area of the house screened off with reduced sensory stimulation, and may contain some calming resources
- The garden.

In public places, the child may access a calm break in some of the following places:

- It may be possible to phone ahead and ask if there is a quiet space available or if somewhere can be set aside for use
- The car, if safe and appropriate
- Toilet cubicle or disabled toilet if it is for a short time.

2. Frequency and time of calm break
   - Schedule calm breaks before and after activities which are likely to be challenging for the child, e.g. groupwork, sensory-based subjects (Art, Music, PE), social events
   - Examine the daily schedule and consider how many calm breaks may be required on that day. If it is a day which consists of several sensory-rich activities, more calm breaks will be required
   - A key factor is flexibility as some days the child will require more breaks and longer breaks than on other days. It is always better to provide too many breaks than too few
   - Additional unscheduled calm breaks can be provided in response to the child's emotional state
   - When calm breaks are included on a schedule, they should always be followed even if the child seems calm, as they can prevent a sudden escalation in anxiety.
3. Requesting a calm break
   - Children with adequate self-awareness who can self-regulate should be encouraged to request calm breaks when they require them. In order to reach the stage of requesting, the individual will need to have insight into what anxiety feels like and relate this to a need for a break
   - A visual prompt card can be used by the child to communicate that a calm break is required
   - It is important to remember that when the student is anxious, the ability to verbally communicate may be compromised, so a visual prompt should be easily accessible.
4. Activities and resources in a calm break

   This will vary for each child depending on what is calming for them.
   - Sitting in a quiet, low stimulation area
   - Calming resources such as music, bubble tubes, weighted items and fidget objects
   - Jigsaws, sudoku, drawing or reading books
   - Proprioceptive activities are calming for many (see section on Proprioceptive activities)
   - Light exercise, such as going for a short walk or bouncing a gym ball
   - Movement, such as rocking, swinging or bouncing
   - Breathing exercises and muscle relaxation may be carried out during calm breaks (see section on these strategies).

Point to remember

The resources and activities used during a calm break will be individualised to each child. Some children benefit from quiet time in a low arousal environment while others require engagement in calming activities, such as physical exercise, deep pressure or breathing exercises. It may take a period of trialling different activities to determine what the child finds effective.

Proprioceptive activities

The receptors for the proprioceptive system are situated in the muscles and joints, and any input to these receptors is regulating. This is because deep pressure input can dampen the high sensitivity to sensory input. Proprioception therefore assists the child in achieving a calm state.

Weightbearing and resistance activities provide heavy load to the muscles and so are often effective in calming people who are experiencing sensory overload. Examples of such activities include:

- Crawling, e.g. through tunnels, under blankets
- Wheelbarrow walks
- Gymnastics
- Jumping
- Lifting weights
- Lying on stomach over exercise ball and weightbearing through arms
- Carrying heavy items
- Pushing and pulling activities
- Stretches with Theraband (a resistive material)
- Squeezing a stress ball or theraputty
- Oral motor activities, e.g. chewing resistive items or sucking thick liquids through a straw

Proprioceptive input can also be incorporated into functional tasks and are sometimes referred to as 'heavy work activities'. These can then teach independence and life skills while helping to provide emotional regulation. Some examples of such tasks in the school setting include setting out chairs in the Assembly Hall, tidying away PE mats and gym equipment or carrying a pile of books to the office.

Weighted items

Deep pressure input is observed to be calming. While light touch is perceived as alerting and potentially harmful, deep pressure input can regulate emotional responses. Some of the proprioceptive activities previously listed are often effective in meeting the need for deep pressure.

Weighted items are frequently used as a calming tool as they provide regulating deep pressure input. Items include weighted blankets, lap pads, belts and vests. Compression vests are another resource used to provide deep pressure input. While these resources can be beneficial as a calming tool, the following points should be considered:

- Request specialist advice from an occupational therapist regarding use of weighted items
- Follow the guidelines regarding what weight is suitable for the weight of the child
- Use for short periods only
- Do not allow the individual to sleep under a weighted blanket
- Consult with a medical professional before using weighted items or a compression vest with individuals who have low muscle tone or breathing complications

Ear defenders

Ear defenders are worn to reduce auditory input, and so tend to be worn in noisy environments or in response to sudden noises. They can be effective in reducing anxiety associated with auditory sensitivities. It is important, however, that they are only used as part of an auditory desensitisation programme. This involves very controlled exposure to noise in order to increase the individual's tolerance of input.

Ear defenders can be used as part of a desensitisation programme by gradually decreasing the amount of time they are worn as the individual becomes more desensitised to noise. The long-term goal is that the ear defenders are eventually removed completely, or only worn in certain circumstances.

Graded exposure or desensitisation

Desensitisation is the term used to describe very gradual and controlled exposure to sensory input which the individual has difficulty in tolerating. The goal is to alter the child's sensitivity to specific input so they are able to cope with it without becoming anxious. It can often be a lengthy process, as the input needs to be increased gradually and must be stopped at the first indicator of distress. The advantage of this strategy is that it makes the individual more able to cope with environmental stimuli, reducing the need for adaptations, which may not always be possible. Additionally, increased tolerance to one type of input often leads to improved responses to other sources of input, for example an individual who is desensitised to different clothing materials may become less sensitive to touching different food textures; or an individual who is desensitised to the sound of the hair dryer may be more able to tolerate the noise of the vacuum cleaner and washing machine.

Key principles to follow when implementing a desensitisation programme are:

- Incremental steps should be small and gradual, e.g. tolerating input for five seconds, then 10 seconds, 15 seconds and so on.
- The individual who is being desensitised to input should be actively involved in planning the programme.
- The individual should have a means of communicating when the input is becoming overwhelming and needs to stop, e.g. provide a visual 'Stop' card.
- Be alert to indicators of distress (e.g. sweating, change in pallor, agitation) and immediately stop activity.
- Use calming strategies during desensitisation activity (e.g. provision of a weighted item, use of calming music) and provide a calm break immediately after activity.
- Praise and celebrate the achievement of each incremental step.

Point to remember

Desensitisation should be a child-led process. The child should be able to request the activity to stop at any time, and should never be persuaded to persist with it when showing indicators of anxiety.

Stress kits

A stress kit, or a calm box, is a practical strategy for supporting emotional regulation at home or school. A child uses the stress kit to reduce feelings of anxiety. It is a proactive intervention to improve self-regulation skills and **it should not be used as a reward**. A stress kit is sometimes effective in reducing anxiety to a level at which the child or young person can then communicate what is causing the anxiety.

The stress kit should be portable. A smaller kit can be kept in a backpack or the car, or smaller items from the kit can be kept in a pocket.

It may include items such as:

- Photograph album containing photos of the child's favourite places/people/pets/cartoon characters etc.
- Calming music on an iPod or similar
- Fidget objects, e.g. blu tac, pencil top, textured ball, paperclip, coins
- Resistance items, e.g. theraband, stress ball

- Weighted items, e.g. weighted lap cushion, weighted belt, weighted blanket
- Fibreoptic lights
- Bubble tube
- Visual items, e.g. spinning top, light-up toy
- Favourite book
- Puzzles (jigsaws, Sudoku, word searches)

Figures 6.6 and 6.7 provide examples of stress kits which can be individualsied depending on preferences and needs.

Figure 6.6 Examples of items for a stress kit

Figure 6.7 Examples of items for a stress kit

Relaxation and mindfulness

Progressive muscle relaxation

Progressive muscle relaxation provides a framework for individuals to go through all the main muscle groups in their body and systematically tense and relax them while breathing slowly.

The child is taught to tense each of the main muscle groups, holding for several seconds and then releasing. The child then works through different muscle groups, for example clenching fists, tensing arm muscles, tensing leg muscles, curling toes. It can be carried out in a specific calm area or in a classroom or home setting.

Relaxation strategies initially need to be taught in a one-to-one setting and at a time when the child is not feeling stressed so that skills can be processed and retained. Visual prompts such as written instructions or a video are useful to support these relaxation activities.

Point to remember

It is important to recognise personal tension spots and early warning signs of anxiety. An adult will need to teach self-awareness of emotions to the autistic child so they are able to identify their early warning signs of anxiety and then engage in a calming activity.

Relaxation should be practised daily. Once techniques have been learnt, students should be able to generalise them to times when they are likely to feel anxious. It is best used as a preventative measure. Children should be encouraged to use their relaxation skills before they go into a situation that they know is going to be stressful and after they have experienced challenging events.

Once the child can recognise that their anxiety has been triggered, they will be better equipped to intervene with coping skills to produce a relaxed response before anxiety increases.

Calm breathing

Calm breathing is a technique that teaches the child to slow down their breathing when feeling stressed or anxious. Anxiety causes breathing to become fast and shallow, which can worsen the feeling of anxiety and lead to breathlessness.

Calm breathing involves taking slow, controlled breaths from the diaphragm. This sends a message to the brain and body that there is no emergency.

Practising and encouraging calm breathing with children can help reduce anxiety and restore a sense of control. Calm breathing is a portable tool that an individual can use in situations when the supporting adult is not there to help.

The skill should first be taught when the person is relaxed, and practised twice a day, with ten breaths reach time, until the skill is mastered. Once a child is comfortable with the breathing technique, it can be transferred to situations that increase or trigger anxiety.

When teaching calm breathing to children use visual supports as they provide a concrete teaching tool and can be used as a visual prompt when the child or young person is feeling anxious.

Mindfulness-based activities

Mindfulness is a technique which helps to focus attention in the present moment and teaches how to refocus when the mind wanders or becomes distressed. It also involves developing a set of attitudinal traits which enhance positive mental health, for example non-judgement, patience, compassion, gratitude and acceptance.

As stated by Mind (2019) the aim is to:

- increase self-awareness
- help you feel calmer and less stressed
- feel more able to choose how to respond to your thoughts and feelings
- cope with difficult thoughts and feelings

Mindfulness can be practised during everyday activities. Exercises are often connected with sensory experiences, for example mindful seeing, listening, eating and walking.

Adapting mindfulness for autism

Emerging literature and research have explored the effectiveness of mindfulness for children with autism. De Bruin et al. (2014) explored how a mindfulness approach could address challenges related to autism which are outlined in Table 6.2.

Research suggests mindfulness increases well-being in children and young people with autism (Hartley et al., 2019) and improves emotional and behaviour functioning, attention and quality of life (Ridderinkhof et al., 2018).

Mindful grounding activity

This technique goes through the five senses to help remind the child of the present. This is a calming technique that can help children and young people when they are anxious.

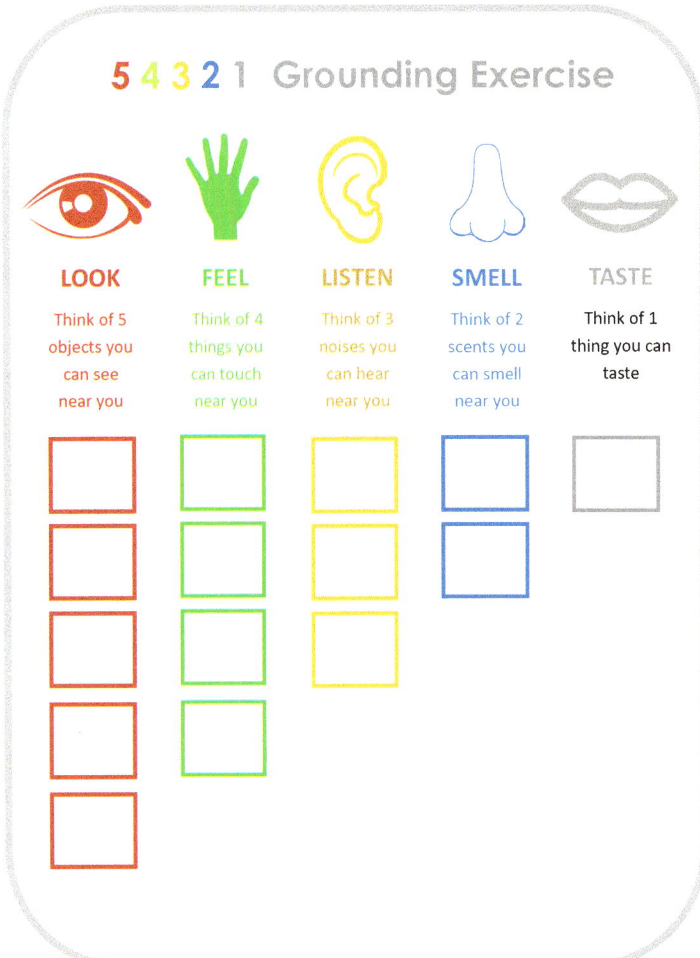

Diagram 6.1 Grounding Activity

Table 6.2 Potential benefits of mindfulness for autistic children and young people

Challenges experienced by children with autism	Core features of mindfulness approach
Poor awareness of self and others	Increase awareness of self and environment
Attention difficulties	Increase attentional control
Internal distractors, e.g. own thoughts	Observe thoughts and let them pass, non-judgementally
External distractors, e.g. sensory	Relating differently to experiences, e.g attitude of beginner's mind non-judgementally
Emotional regulation – alexithymia and reactivity	Improve awareness of feelings and response
High rates of stress	Letting go and responding with awareness

Body scan

A body scan is a guided, mindful activity to help the child shift their attention to different parts of the body, while noticing any sensations experienced (e.g. tingling, warmth, pulsating, tightness etc.) without judging the experiences as good or bad. This technique is effective in a variety of situations and can be carried out in a comfortable seated position. The body scan technique can be helpful in settling to sleep.

Mindful breathing

Paying attention to the breath has a different focus than calm breathing. The focus in mindful breathing is not on changing the rate to induce relaxation, but instead, to use the natural rhythm of the breath as an anchor to practise 'returning' attention to the present moment and away from distracting thoughts.

Guided imagery/visualisation

Studies have shown that regular relaxation is one of the most effective treatments for anxiety (Weisz et al., 2006). Visualisation can help individuals with autism manage their anxiety in stressful situations. Steps for guided imagery include:

- Go to your relaxing place and use your relaxation rhyme
- Look at the picture of your relaxing place
- Do your breathing exercises
- Feel your body relax

The happiness switch

www.relaxkids.com/

1. Remember a time you felt happy. It might be when you were with your family, laughing or doing something that really made you proud of yourself.
2. Take your mind back to that place and try and imagine you are back there and see what you saw and hear what you heard and remember how great you felt.
3. As you think about the memory, try and make the colours in the memory brighter and make the sounds louder.
4. Now, squeeze thumb and first finger together on your right hand as you think about your happy memory.
5. Next time you are feeling lonely or sad, just squeeze your thumb and first finger and remember your happy memory. This is your happy switch and you can use it whenever you need to relax or feel better.

Section two

Cognitive Behaviour Therapy (CBT) based strategies for anxiety management. These strategies are longer term approaches and involve addressing how the child/young person thinks about the anxieties they face.

CBT is shown to be effective in changing the way we think and respond behaviourally to emotions such as anxiety, anger and sadness.

How does CBT work?

CBT is designed to help people notice and understand the connections between how their thoughts, behaviours and emotions affect each other. It is used to support the person to learn new ways of thinking about and responding to situations that they find distressing.

We know that not all our thoughts are accurate, but we often accept our thinking patterns as true without questioning them. This can result in the development of inaccurate and unhelpful thinking patterns that can impact how we respond and interact with people or the world around us. CBT encourages the individual to stop and check their thinking and explore other more realistic and accurate ways of consideration.

When we experience heightened anxiety our negative thoughts occur more often and can seem overwhelming. CBT teaches children strategies to help control these thoughts. It is not enough to tell someone to stop worrying or stop unpleasant and scary thoughts. This is hard to do and sometimes the negative thoughts can seem stronger when the child tries to stop them.

CBT in autism

Research indicates that autistic children can benefit from participating in CBT, and this can lead to a reduction in both the experience of anxiety and in coping strategies to respond to anxiety (Alhers et al., 2017; Reaven et al, 2012; Spain et al., 2015; Storch et al., 2012; Sukhodolosky et al, 2013; Ung et al., 2015; Vasa et al., 2014; Wood et al., 2009).

These studies highlight that small modifications to CBT delivery increases its effectiveness for autistic service users. Methods used should be more concrete and visually based.

The use of modified CBT for autistic young people has been reinforced by the National Institute for Clinical Excellence (NICE) (guidelines updated 2013). NICE states adaptations to the delivery of cognitive and behavioural interventions for autistic service users should include:

- emotion recognition training
- a more concrete and structured approach with a greater use of written and visual information, which may include worksheets, thought bubbles, images and 'tool boxes'

- a greater emphasis on changing behaviour, rather than cognitions, and using the behaviour as the starting point for intervention
- making rules explicit and explaining their context
- simplified cognitive activities, for example using multiple-choice worksheets
- involving a family member, carer or professional (with the consent of the autistic person) to support the implementation of an intervention
- maintaining the person's attention by offering regular breaks, especially if the person is sensory hyper- or hypo-reactive
- incorporating special interests into therapy if possible

Note: the guidelines do not appear to give specific guidance for those with autism and coexisting mental disorders and/or a learning disability.

There are several cognitive-based strategies which can be used by autistic children to help them control their negative thoughts and reactions:

1. Distraction Techniques

The aim of distraction techniques is to support the individual to control distressing thoughts by thinking about something else. Engaging the brain in activities which require concentration helps to keep it busy, so there is less capacity for anxious thoughts.

Some useful distraction techniques include:

- Listening to music
- Doing a crossword puzzle or sudoku
- Reading a book, comic or magazine
- Engaging in a physical activity which requires concentration, or counting
- Counting objects in the surrounding environment, e.g. chairs, people, plug sockets, cars
- LEGO or other types of visual methodical activities

Thinking puzzles (Stallard, 2002): Examples include counting backwards from 100 in 5s, spelling the names of family members backwards, listing all players of a favourite sports team.

Point to remember

Use the child's special interest in distraction techniques as this provides familiarity which will calm them further. For example, if the child has a special interest in planets, a thinking puzzle could involve spelling the names of planets backwards.

2. Cognitive Restructuring
   - Cognitive restructuring is a technique which helps children identify, challenge and change anxiety inducing thoughts and beliefs. Many autistic people are anxious due to distorted and negative thoughts, such as over-focus on the negative aspects of an event, predicting that something will be difficult, magnifying small problems or assuming that feelings are facts. Cognitive restructuring aims to replace these negative distortions with more accurate ways of thinking. The process involves:
   - Awareness of negative thoughts
   - Questioning the accuracy of the thoughts
   - Evaluating the evidence for the thoughts
   - Testing out the new thoughts

Cognitive restructuring can be made more concrete and visual for autistic children through *A Poison Thought* game (available on www.autismteachingstrategies.com). Negative thoughts are written in red thought bubbles, and new thoughts which challenge the negative thinking are placed in green thought bubbles. The red bubbles can be seen as the poison and the green bubbles are the antidotes.

The adult can create pre-written thought bubbles that may cover many of the most common problem thoughts of their child or pupil. The child can also be provided with blank thought bubbles to fill in their own poison thoughts.

Some children feel anxious because they have thoughts that bad things will happen to them or to people they love. It is important to remind children that although these thoughts are unpleasant, they **are not facts**.

Point to remember

It can be difficult to identify and communicate what your thoughts are. Drawing or role playing with puppets/figurines can help identify negative thoughts.

It can also be hard to recognise what thought errors (cognitive distortions) you are making. Most people benefit from having an independent person or therapist who can support them to do this.

Diagram 6.2

3. Cognitive Coping Cards

Cognitive coping cards provide short sentences prompting coping skills the individual can use when experiencing anxiety. The cards are portable reminders of how to control anxiety. They usually contain a mixture of psychoeducation, coping statements and skills:

- ➢ Psychoeducation on anxiety; that is the common symptoms the person experiences.
- ➢ A reminder that physical symptoms (e.g. sweaty palms, stomach-aches) are just anxiety and not a sign of something more serious.
- ➢ Coping statements to help them reframe their anxious thoughts, e.g. I get everything wrong but I can ask for help and do this thing right.
- ➢ Positive coaching statements or self-talk (e.g. 'I can get through this!').

- A reminder to use some coping skills (e.g. I can do relaxed breathing).
- Some calming facts your student has used before, e.g. It may be hard, but if I stay calm and remember help is available, I will be okay.

(www.anxietybc.com)

Coping statements

Cognitive coping cards normally include 'coping self-talk', i.e. instead of listening to your negative thoughts, your doubts and worries you replace them with coping statements. This technique is helpful as it can help stop the stream of negative thoughts which often increase anxious or sad feelings. Replacing these negative thoughts with coping self-talk can help the person feel more relaxed; increase feelings of self-esteem and confidence; and motivates the person to try rather than avoid.

Some children and young people with autism can have a negative self-image and fail to see their strengths. Positive self-talk is a way of encouraging and reminding them of their achievements and things they do well. The aim of positive self-talk is to help you understand that although you may not be doing something 100% perfectly, you are doing it better than your negative thoughts are allowing you to think.

Involving peers in group/class work which celebrates difference is key in building awareness and understanding, of not just the strengths of autistic individuals, but also of their peers. Acknowledging that everyone has different strengths, that everyone finds some things difficult, and some things easier, is a starting point for either open discussion or small group discussions. Not only will this help to build confidence and self-esteem but it helps them to believe in themselves, and develop their resilience. Encourage an appreciation that we are all different, and being different is good and should be celebrated and supported.

Self-regulation

Helping children to manage their emotions, across all ages, is vital. It is particularly important approaching the adolescent years when there are more social and communication pressures placed upon them. Helping children to identify and recognise their emotions and feelings is paramount to helping them cope with anxiety-provoking situations. For example, talking about how their body feels when they are anxious, as it is possible that they will not have connected the physical sensation (e.g. having a sore stomach, feeling nauseous, light headed or having sweaty hands) with the emotion of anxiety.

Affective education

Affective education is a curriculum designed to help children understand their emotional and social behaviour. It encourages them to understand emotions in both themselves and in others; in order to facilitate control of emotions we first need to recognise and understand them, before we can change them.

Children need to learn why we have emotions, their basic functions, and be able to identify different levels of emotions. We need to teach children that anxiety is normal: all humans have evolved to experience fear in certain situations to keep us safe from danger. Anxiety is the feeling you get when you have worries that you can't stop thinking about. Children may feel anxious about something that has already happened or anxious about something that will happen in the future.

When teaching autistic children about emotions, start with one emotion at a time, begin with simple emotions such as happiness before moving on to more complex emotions such as anxiety and anger. Affective education includes teaching the individual how various emotions will affect their bodies, their thinking and the way in which they behave.

Resources to support this teaching include

- The STAMP Treatment Manual – *Exploring Feelings for Young Children with High Functioning Autism or Asperger's Disorder*
- *Feelings and Emotions (50 Cards) Emotional Literacy, Discussion and Enquiry* by Smart Kids
- *Miniland Emotiblocks Basic Emotions*
- Kids Create *Learn Your Emotions Magnetic Game*
- App – *Feelings with Milo* by Doonan Speech Therapy
- App – *Emotions Collection* by itbook
- App – *Autism Emotion* by ModelMe Kids

Recognising emotions

Autistic children need to be taught the relevant cues which indicate different emotions, this includes facial expressions, tone of voice, body language or actions. They may experience difficulty interpreting emotions from a person's facial expression or tone of voice. They may not identify relevant non-verbal cues or can misinterpret cues, for example a loud voice does not always mean the person is angry, nor do tears always mean a person is experiencing sadness.

Point to remember

Parents/educators need to teach individuals with autism the language of emotion, that is what it feels like to be worried, angry, sad, frustrated.

Beginning with simple emotions, teach the individual what the emotion looks and feels like.

What does anxiety feel like?

- Feeling sick
- Red face
- 'Butterflies'?
- Shortness of breath
- Want to run away
- Quick heartbeat
- Too many thoughts
- Crying
- Dizzy

What does anger feel like?

- Shouting and yelling
- Using bad words
- Throwing things
- Breaking things
- Hitting, kicking fighting
- Wanting to hurt yourself

Use the Body Outline Worksheet (Resource 10) to support the individual with identifying physiological symptoms experienced with various emotions.

The Body Outline Worksheet is especially effective for autistic children. It helps to increase their awareness of how their bodies respond to feelings such as anxiety, anger and sadness. This is a visual method which supports an autistic person with communicating their individual physiological response to feelings.

Some strategies for supporting understanding emotions include:

- Picture cards – illustrations of people's faces expressing different emotions
- Social Stories™ – Social Stories™ (see Section One)
- Emotions bingo – one person reads out a situation card and the others guess the emotion, when the correct emotion is identified players cover the emotion picture with a bingo chip
- Facial recognitions – picture cards, photographs of family/friends, magazines, cartoon characters
- Feelings book – incorporate the child's own name and photos into any personal materials to make it individualised and more relevant. When the child can be mindful of their own emotions, they can begin to manage their behaviours surrounding them and communicate better about emotional states. This includes story-telling and learning cause–effect relations, for example 'he is mad because he lost the game'.
- Modelling – supporting adult displays appropriate emotional behaviour for the child to model; encourage the individual to practise in a mirror
- Games – many games and activities to help autistic children learn about emotions in a way that engages them (online games and apps available), for example Do2learn; Symbol word, Chill Panda
- Creative role-play with puppets – using puppets can be a great way to learn and practise social responses and assess emotions. Create a trigger event, for example losing a game or breaking something, a situation which triggers an emotional response and discuss the character's reactions to the event. It's best to help organise the storyline with the individual and designate roles. The child might do well as the 'friend' puppet and you can instruct them on how to 'be a good friend' and ask, 'What would you say to your friend who is sad?' This can be paired with comic strip conversations to create a visual depiction of the conversation or interaction.

Point to remember

Developing visual supports, which are both cognitively and age appropriate (using images on cards or on an iPad), can help to improve knowledge of facial expressions, and understanding of the associated physical signs of emotions such as anxiety. This again should be taught on a one-to-one basis, when the individual is in a calm and alert state for learning.

Identifying anxiety and levels of distress

Teach the child to recognise the signs of anxiety relevant to him/her (e.g. breathing more quickly, feeling flushed or warm, sweating, loss of concentration, irritability, desire to escape the situation, nausea). This is often best taught using a diagram of the body (as shown previously) and labelling the physiological signs of stress in different parts of the body. It is likely to be easier for an autistic child to recognise these concrete signs of anxiety once they are taught than to understand the emotions initially.

Support the child to identify personal triggers for his/her anxiety. Some children feel anxious about something very particular, for example other crying children, men with beards. Some children feel anxious separating from their parents or meeting new people. Some are anxious about going to new places or going to environments which may be crowded, for example supermarkets. Some children are anxious about changes in their routine; they may check with you by asking questions repeatedly because they worry the routine will change unexpectedly. Some children worry about activities or places because of sensory input which is overwhelming or painful for them, for example nail cutting, hair cutting, fire alarms, hand dryers in public toilets.

The child then knows to be alert for signs of anxiety in these environments/activities and to be prepared to use calming strategies.

We must help children understand who or what their triggers are and when they are likely to happen. We should encourage and teach a visual communication system so the person can describe how they are feeling rather than simply asking them (for example emotion thermometer – add link), as we know individuals with autism can find both receptive and expressive communication difficult, particularly during periods of distress.

Remember, there can be differences in anxiety presentation for girls and boys with autism. Unpredictable explosive behaviour is regarded as a typical autistic response to anxiety. However, where boys are inclined to explode, girls may be more likely to implode, internalising the anxiety.

Point to remember

Ensure all school staff are informed about the presentation of autism in girls. This may help girls who can be 'suffering in silence', as their anxiety can be identified and addressed.

Communicating anxiety

Teaching explicit communication and interaction skills is important, even amongst those girls who may present as being proficient in communicating. There are different ways an autistic individual can be taught to communicate their anxiety. The strategy you teach will depend on the person's age and developmental ability. Some individuals like to use emotion cards or break cards to communicate to an adult they are feeling anxious. Other people may not wish to use an obvious prompt in front of others, so you may need to provide a more discrete method. For example, coloured pens to represent anxiety are useful for adolescents or young people who are self-aware. They can hold or flash a red pen to their teacher to indicate that they need a break. When using this method the individual can effectively communicate their anxiety without drawing attention to him or herself or letting others know what he or she is communicating.

Emotion thermometers

Emotion thermometers can be presented in many formats; some use numbers to rate emotions while others use colours, words or symbols. It is important to choose the format which the autistic individual can best relate to.

Emotion thermometers are a visual communication tool used to support an autistic individual to describe and/or rate the level of emotions. The person can use the emotion thermometer to visually indicate if he/she is becoming anxious, and the level of intensity of the anxiety. Depending on the level of anxiety indicated, the parent or education professional can encourage the autistic individual to access an appropriate calming strategy.

These visual communication strategies can be adapted to suit the individual's special interest, which may promote motivation and engagement.

Emotion thermometers and the Incredible 5 Point Scale are effective tools for supporting an individual with communicating an emotion, such as anxiety. It also provides a means of identifying the level of intensity of their anxiety at any given time. It can help a person build up their language of anxiety and support accurate expression of how they are feeling. This will help the individual generalise the language and skills across situations and environments.

Point to remember

Ensure the emotion thermometer used by the individual is portable and that all staff working with the child know how it is used. Staff should also be familiar with the appropriate actions for each level of the thermometer, i.e. what to offer the child when mildly, moderately or severely anxious.

Emotion ladder or traffic light

Create an 'emotion ladder' consisting of green, amber and red. Green usually indicates that all is good or 'I feel ok', amber indicates 'I am starting to feel nervous' and red shows 'I am anxious'.

Children place their name/photo somewhere on the ladder depending on how they are feeling. This strategy enables children to show you how they are feeling at a given moment and is not dependent on expressive language.

It is helpful to have strategies visually displayed to the side or under each rung of the ladder so children can see what they can do to help them get back to green 'I feel ok'. Strategies can include breathing techniques (taking deep breaths by counting slowly to three), using a calm break token (for a younger child at primary or special school) or a young person in post-primary school may prefer to discretely raise a coloured pen to indicate the need to leave the room or speak to a teacher.

Incredible 5-Point scale

www.5pointscale.com/

The Incredible 5-Point Scale provides a visual breakdown of anxiety and includes individualised anxiety strategies for each stage, and directs the child to a strategy based on their reported level of anxiety. The 5-Point Scale was developed by Kari Dunn Buron, who is a specialist teacher from Minnesota, USA. It is described as an antecedent-based cognitive behavioural intervention that teaches social information and emotional regulation in a systematic way using visuals.

When using the Incredible 5-Point Scale the following points should be borne in mind:

- Be positive
- Break a concept or idea into five parts
- Teach skills

A special interest should, where possible, be incorporated. For example, types of dinosaur or insect, or even a volcano to indicate building anger. The Scale doesn't necessarily need to be solely visual.

Self prompt regulation cards

After teaching the individual about various emotions including anxiety and anger, provide small portable emotion cue cards. These should be portable so the person can carry them around: they act as a visual reminder of which strategies they can use when they are feeling distressed.

Initially the supporting adult will likely need to prompt the autistic individual to look at their cue card when they recognise the person is becoming anxious. However, as you continue to teach about recognising their own anxiety, the person will become better at using their cue cards independently.

Positively reinforce the child or young person for successful use of communication supports. Everyone likes to gain positive feedback whether it be at home, school or work environment. The need to gain positive feedback is no different for individuals with autism, as like everyone else positive feedback helps to build self-esteem and confidence. By telling the child or young person what they did well this will help to build their confidence, particularly in social situations. It can help reinforce the socially expected, appropriate behaviour for the individual and reduce the level of anxiety they may experience.

Co-regulation

Some autistic children may not be able to independently access emotionally regulating activities/resources or communicate their needs with others. In some cases, they may not be aware of their own emotions, or link anxiety symptoms to the need for regulating activities. Some may eventually develop these skills through affective education, while others might not yet be ready to engage in this type of intervention programme. In these instances, the adult (parent or professional), needs to take the responsibility for emotional regulation, sometimes referred to as co-regulation.

Point to remember

Affective education will take time to be effective, and so in the meantime, parents or professionals will need to regulate the child by being observant of their emotions and providing emotionally regulating input.

Identifying triggers

The adult should be cognisant of what might trigger the child's anxiety, and be ready to offer regulating input in the presence of such triggers. If it is a planned or expected trigger, such as going to Assembly or engaging in a social event, calming input should be planned in advance, and calm breaks added to the visual schedule. If it is an unexpected trigger, such as a loud noise or a sudden change to routine, the adult should observe the child's response and offer appropriate calming input as required.

Identifying emotions

The adult who is supporting the child should be observant of the signs and symptoms of anxiety. These are often obvious, but at other times, may be very specific to the child, and only someone who knows the child well may recognise their individual signs of stress. It is advisable to have a written record of the child's triggers and signs of anxiety so that if other adults are working with the child, they can be aware of these. There may be physiological signs, such as sweating, change in pallor or shaking, or behavioural signs, such as escalation in repetitive behaviours, oppositional behaviour, cursing or trying to get out of the room.

Regulation of emotions

If supporting adults feel there is a risk the child could become anxious, or if they observe signs of anxiety, they should provide calming input. This may involve using a visual support to direct the child to a calm area, or to prompt them to engage in a calming activity. Some children, however, in a heightened state of anxiety may not be able to process and follow the visual prompt, or they may not be calm enough to transition to a calm area. In these instances, the calming input is brought to them. The teacher or parent, for example, may bring a calming resource known to be effective with the child, such as a weighted blanket, calming music or blowing bubbles.

Point to remember

Calming resources should be introduced to autistic children when they are calm so they become comfortable with the resource and then it is familiar to them when used in episodes of anxiety. A new resource should not be introduced when the child is already stressed as this could escalate the anxiety.

An adult can also co-regulate the child by using minimal verbal language, using a quiet voice and maintaining a calm demeanour.

Conclusion

The best anxiety management strategy is prevention. Preventative strategies are effective for the autistic child; they can build resilience through understanding and managing potential triggers. Prevention reduces the risk of the child becoming upset, losing confidence and learning unhelpful coping strategies. We promote prevention by developing an understanding of where the difficulties may occur and building strengths and resilience. Providing structured visual environments, providing predictability when possible and removing uncertainty all build into preventative strategies.

Where an anxiety response is unavoidable our best strategies in a moment of crisis are to try and divert and distract the child using interesting or favoured tasks or games. There is a temptation to try to coax or persuade an anxious person out of their response and this is not always helpful. It often is best to reduce verbal input and to redirect to a task and to keep verbal input at a minimum until the child has recovered.

This resource taken in its totality provides the context to begin to understand the individual experience. It stresses the importance of observation and assessment whether informal or formal and provides a range of strategies that are both evidence- and practice- based. It can be used in its totality and also as a reference for parents and teachers who seek a practical support for planning to reduce the likelihood of an anxious response and to manage anxiety once it has been triggered. This resource was written by experienced practitioners with a focus on the practical in the hope that shared practice and experience can foster the skills and create environments that provide competent support for autistic children and young people.

References

Alhers, K., Gabrielsen, D., Lewis, D., Brady, A. M., & Lichford, A. (2017). Supporting individuals with autism spectrum disorder in understanding and coping with complex social emotional issues. *School Psychology International*, 38 (6), 586–607.

Crozier, S., & Tincani, M. (2007). Effects of Social Stories™ on prosocial behaviour of pre-school children with autism spectrum disorder. *Journal of Autism and Developmental Disorders*, 37 (9), 1803–1814.

De Bruin, E., Blom, R., Smit, F., van Steensel, F., & Bogels, S. (2014). MYmind: Mindfulness training for youngsters with autism spectrum disorders and their parents. *Autism*, 19 (8), 906–914.

Delano, M., & Snell, M. (2006). The effects of Social Stories™ on the social engagement of children with autism. *Journal of Positive Behaviour Interventions*, 8 (1), 29–42.

Gray, C. (1994). *The New Social Stories Book*. Arlington, TX: . Future Horizons.

Gray, C. (2018). The social story philosophy taken from https://carolgraysocialstories.com/wp-content/uploads/2018/12/Social-Stories-10.2-Criteria.pdf Accessed 2 December 2019.

Hartley, M., Darslyn, D., & Due, C. (2019). Mindfulness for children and adults with autism spectrum disorder and their caregivers: A meta-analysis. *Journal of Autism and Developmental Disorders*, 49 (2), 4306–4319.

National Institute for Health and Care Excellence. (2013). Autism spectrum disorder in under 19s: Support and management. www.nice.org.uk/guidance/cg170/chapter/1-Recommendations Accessed 2 December 2019.

Reaven, J., Blakeley-Smith, A., Culhane-Shelburne, K., & Hepburn, S. (2012). Group cognitive behavior therapy for children with high-functioning autism spectrum disorders and anxiety: A randomized trial. *Journal of Child Psychology & Psychiatry*, 53 (4), 410–419.

Reynhout, G., & Carter, M. (2009). The use of Social Stories™ by teachers and their perceived efficacy. *Research in Autism Spectrum Disorders*, 3 (1), 232–251.

Ridderinkhof, E., de Bruin, E., van Sen Driesschen, S., & Bogel, S. (2018). Attention in children with autism spectrum disorder and the effects of a mindfulness-based program. *Journal of Attention Disorders*, 18, 681–692.

Scattone, D., Tingstom, D., & Wilczynsky, S. (2006). increasing appropriate social interactions of children with autism spectrum disorders using Social Stories™. *Focus on Autism and Developmental Disabilities*, 21 (4), 211–222.

Spain, D., Sin, J., Chalder, T., Murphy, D., & Happe, F. (2015). Cognitive behaviour therapy for adults with autism spectrum disorders and psychiatric co-morbidity: A review. *Research in Autism Spectrum Disorders*, 9 (1), 151–162.

Stallard, P. (2002). *Think Good Feel Good. A Cognitive Behavioural Workbook for Young Children*. Wiley-Blackwell. Hoboken, NJ.

Storch, E., Arnold, E., Jones, A., Ale, C., Wood, J., & Ehrenreich-May, J. (2012). The role of co-occurring disruptive behavior in the clinical presentation of children and adolescents with anxiety in the context of autism spectrum disorders. *Child Psychiatry & Human Development*, 43 (5), 734–746.

Sukhodolosky, D. G., Bloch, M. H., Panza, K. E., & Reichow, B. (2013). Cognitive-behavioral therapy for anxiety in children with high functioning autism: A meta-analysis. *Pediatrics*, 132, 1341–1350.

Ung, D., Selles, R., Small, B., & Storch, E. (2015). A systematic review and meta-analysis of cognitive-behavioral therapy for anxiety in youth with high-functioning autism spectrum disorders. *Child Psychiatry and Human Development*, 46 (4), 533–547.

Vasa, R., Carroll, L., Nozzolillo, A., Mahajan, R., Mazurek, M., & Bennett, A. (2014). A systematic review of treatments for anxiety in youth with autism spectrum disorders. *Journal of Autism and Developmental Disorders*, 44 (12), 3215–3229.

Weisz, J., McCarty, C., & Valeri, S. (2006). Effects of psychotherapy for depression in children and adolescents: A meta-analysis. *Psychological Bulletin*, 132 (1), 132–149.

Wood, J., Drahota, A., Sze, K., Har, K., Chiu, A., & Langer, D. (2009). Cognitive behavioral therapy for anxiety in children with autism spectrum disorders: A randomized, controlled trial. *Journal of Child Psychology and Psychiatry and Allied Disciplines*, 50 (3), 224–234.

Resource 1: Visual schedule for school (symbol plus word)

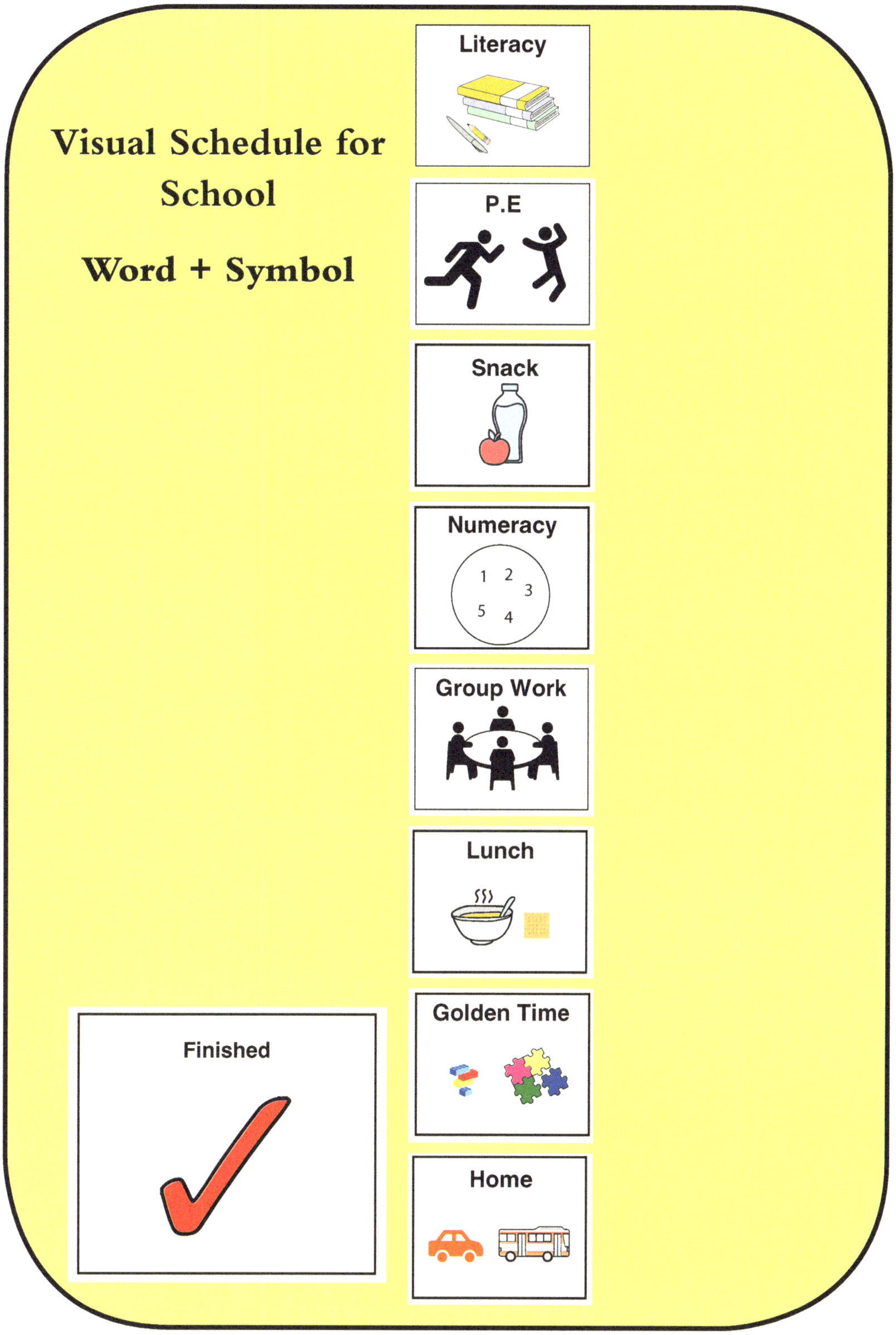

Resource 2: Break out cards

I need a
"Quick 10"
break

I need 1
minute,
please

I need 2
minutes,
please

I need 5
minutes,
please

May I please
be excused?

Resource 3:
Calm corner tokens

Calm Corner Tokens

Resource 4:
Muscle relaxation step by step

Muscle Relaxation Routine

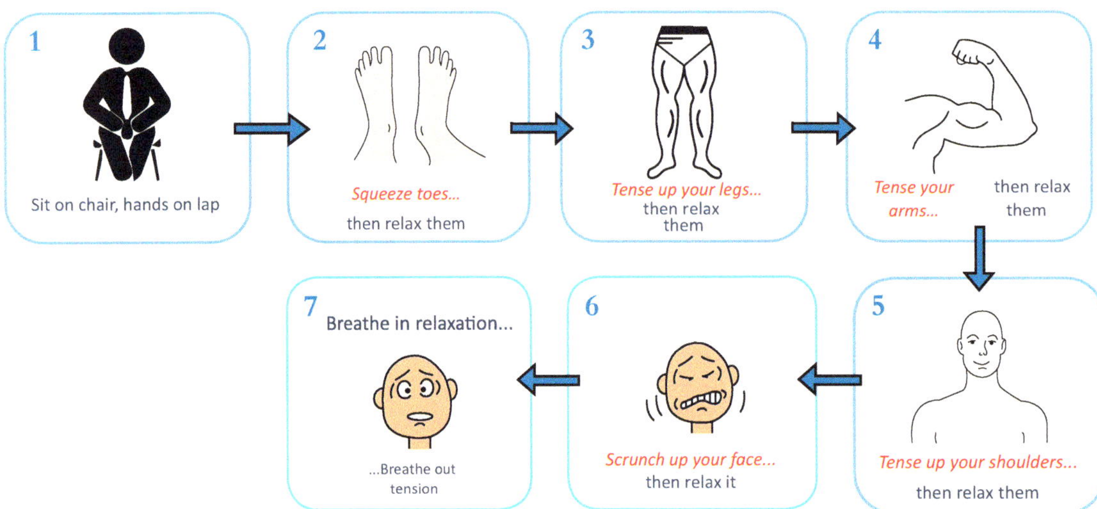

Muscle Relaxation Routine

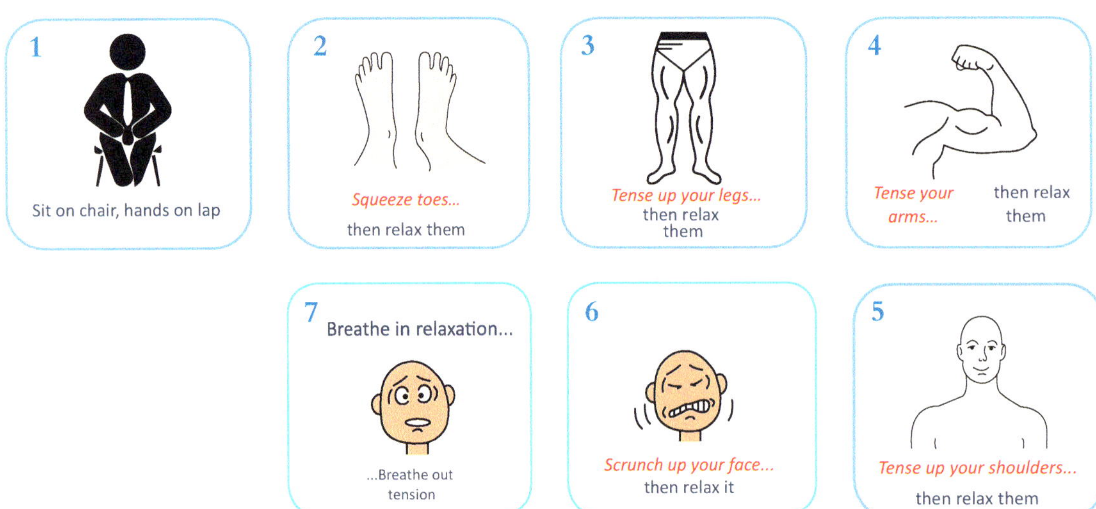

Resource 5: Relaxation breathing

Relaxation Breathing

Resource 5:
(*Continued*)

Relaxation Breathing

Smell the flower

Breathe in...

Blow the dandelions

Breathe out...

Resource 5:
(*Continued*)

Relaxation Breathing

Smell the hot chocolate

Breathe in...

Blow the bubbles

Breathe out...

Resource 5:
(*Continued*)

Relaxation Breathing

Blow the bubbles

Breathe out...

Resource 6: Square breathing

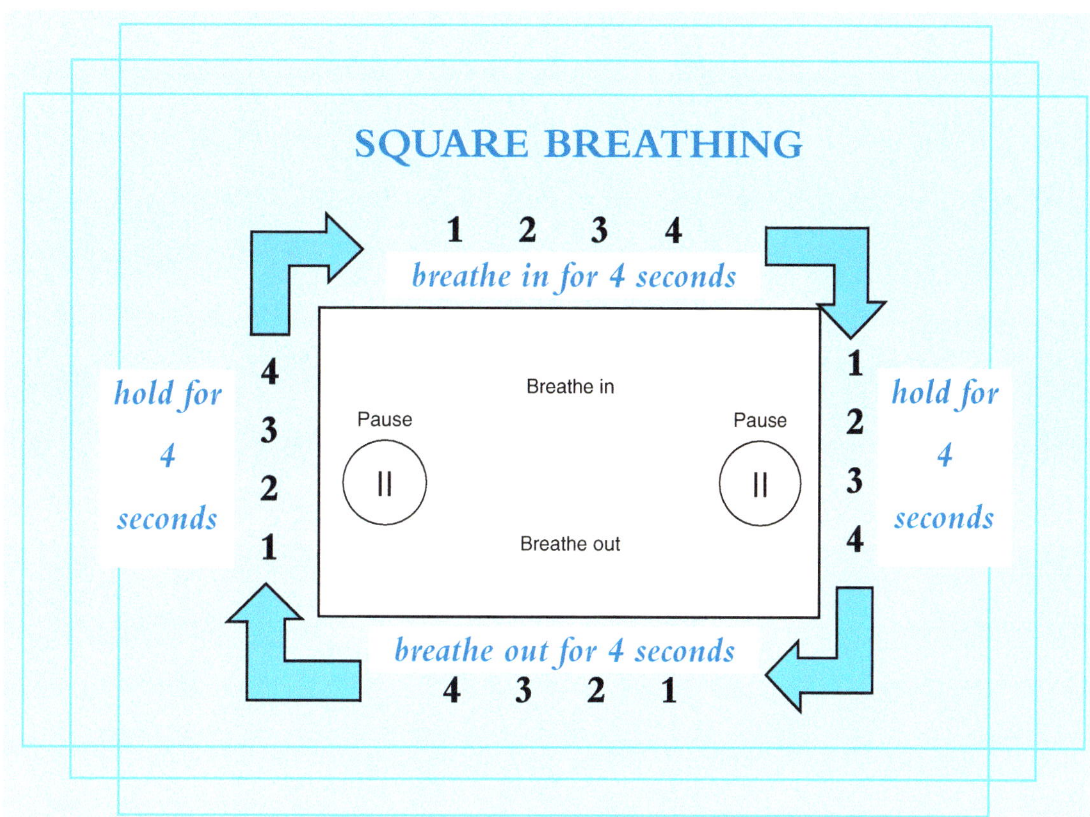

Resource 7: Star breathing

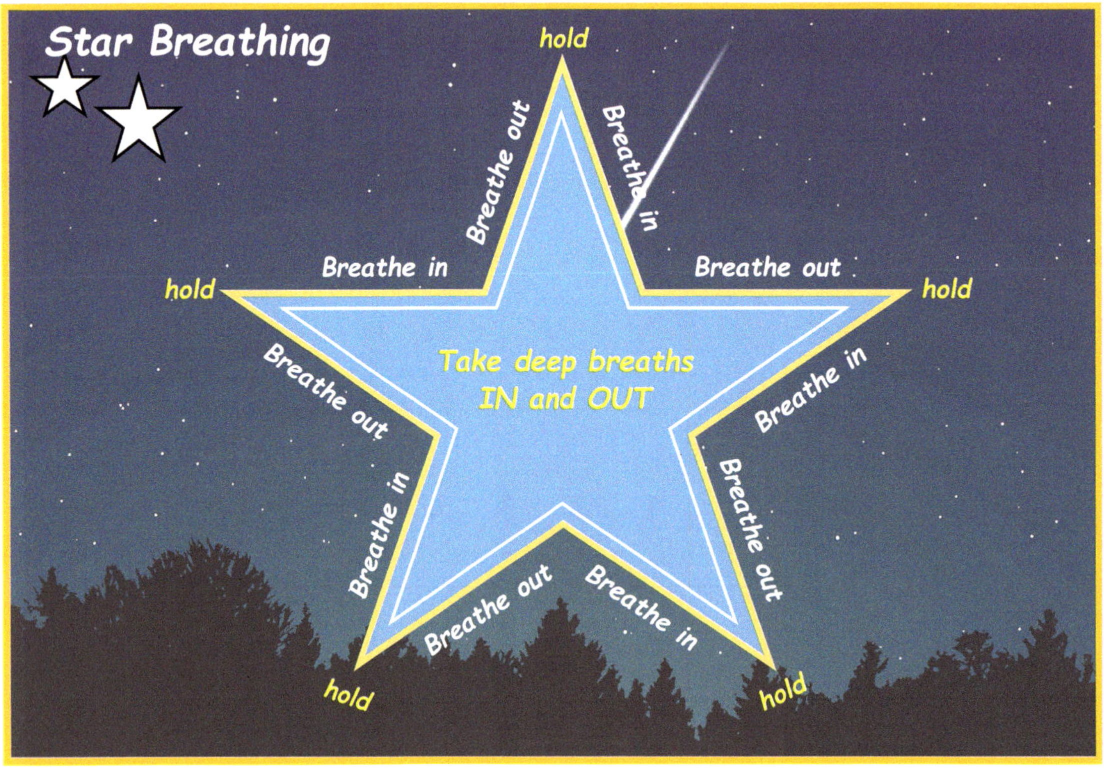

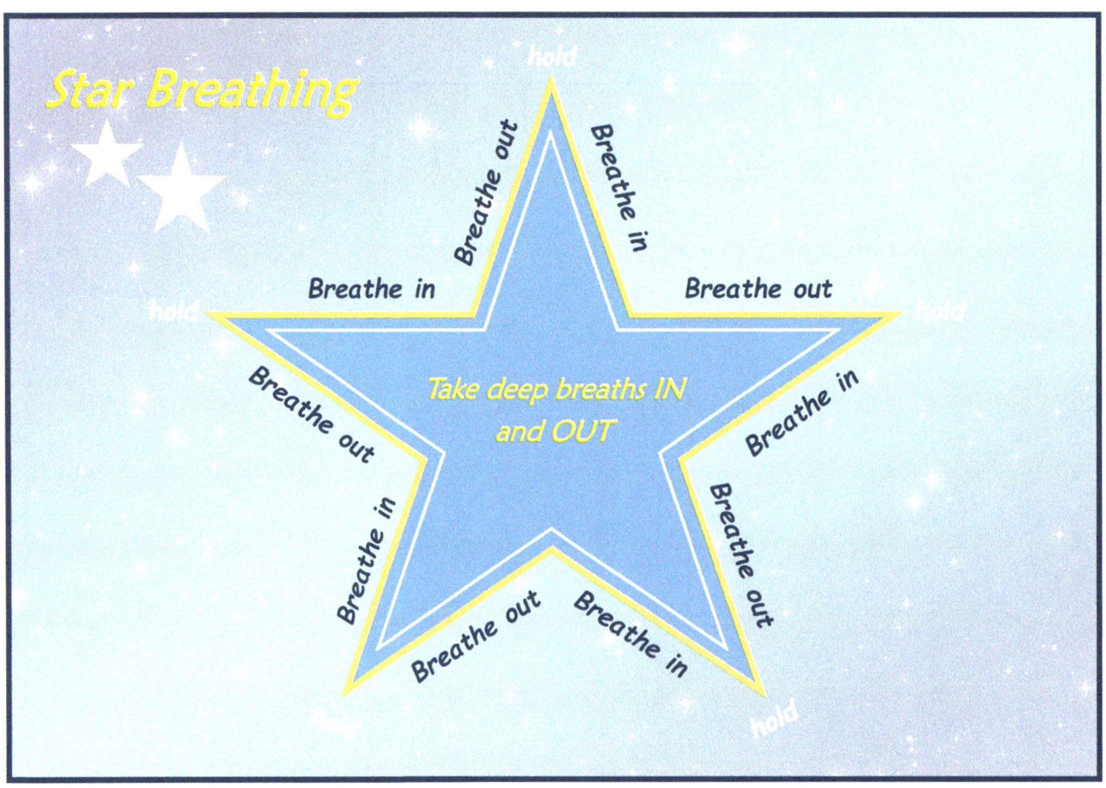

Resource 8: Ocean breaths

Resource 8: Rainbow breaths

Resource 8: Butterfly breaths

Resource 9: Count 1–10

Resource 10: Body scan

Resource 11: Feelings thermometer

Resource 11:
(*Continued*)

Resource 12: Feelings speedometer

Resource 13: Feelings chart

My Feelings Chart

	How do I feel?	What can I do?
5	 I need some help!	□ □ □ □
4	 I'm really upset	□ □ □ □
3	 I've got a problem	□ □ □ □
2	 Things are pretty good	□ □ □ □
1	 Feeling great!	□ □ □ □

Resource 14: Looks/Sounds like rating scale

Rating	Looks/Sounds like	Feels like	I Can Try
5			
4			
3			
2			
1			

Resource 15:
Feelings volcano

Resource 16: Traffic lights

Resource 17: How am I feeling?

Resource 18: When I am frustrated

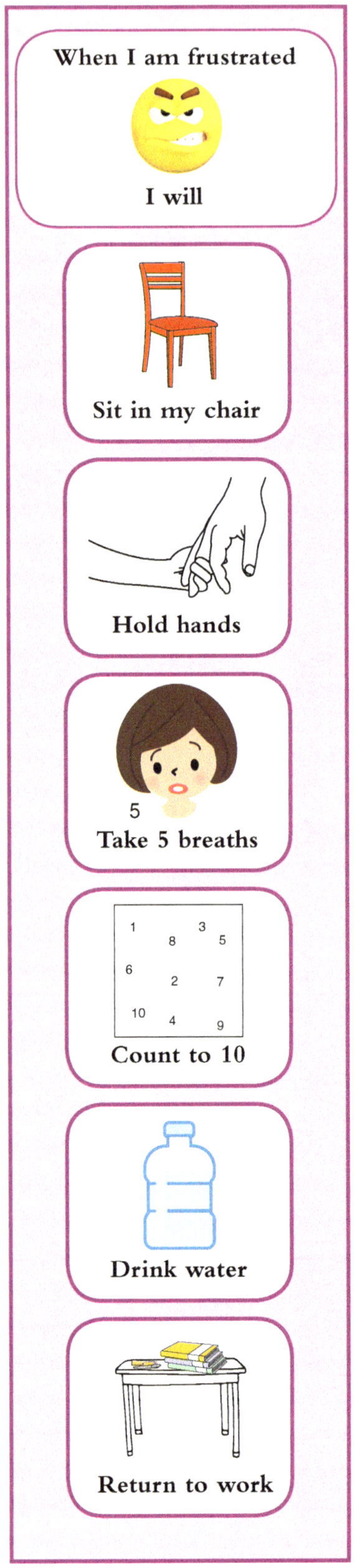

Resource 18:
(*Continued*)

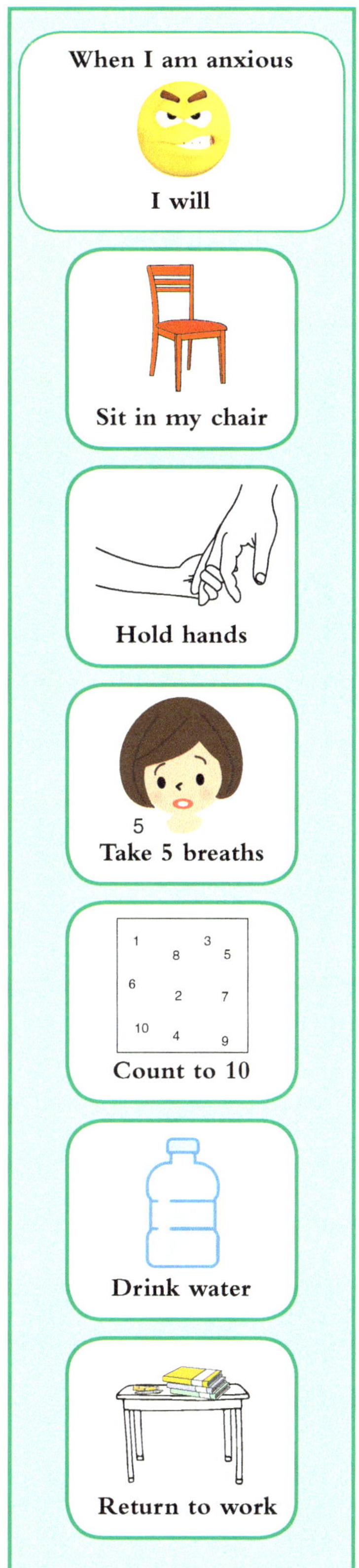

Resource 19: When I need help

WHEN I NEED HELP

If I don't understand I can...

- Re-read the instructions

- Quietly ask a friend for help

- Ask the teacher for help

Resource 19:
(*Continued*)

WHEN I NEED HELP

If I'm frustrated or stressed...

- I can walk away or ignore

- I can ask for a break

- I can find an adult to ask for help

Resource 20: Anger management cards

Anger Management Cards

Anger Management Cards

Anger Management Cards

Anger Management Cards

Resource 21: How do I feel?

How do I feel?

happy

excited

sad

confused

worried/anxious

upset/cross

angry

very angry

I may need to choose a calming activity

Resource 22:
Chill skills for younger children

Chill Skills for Younger Children

Fizzy Lemonade

Jump up and down or shake your body as fast as you can for as long as possible. Now, stop and feel your body fizzing like lemonade.

This exercise helps you feel the energy in your body and helps you to notice the difference between moving and relaxing.

Butterflies

Give yourself a massage and let your finger lightly flutter like a butterfly all over your face, neck, chest and arms.

This exercise shows you how a gentle massage can help you feel better.

Pencil

Stand or sit up tall, with your legs together. Raise your arms above your head and clasp your thumbs together with your fingers pointing upwards. Stand very tall and stretch your whole body, squeezing your legs as tight as you can. After about 10 seconds of squeezing tight, let your arms go and relax.

This exercise shows you how a good stretch held for a few seconds can help you feel relaxed and energised.

Thumb Massage

Hold your left hand with your right hand, placing your right thumb in the middle of your left palm. Very gently, stroke and circle your thumb around your palm.

This exercise is to help you feel relaxed. You can do this whenever you are feeling stressed or anxious.

Resource 22:
(*Continued*)

Chill Skills for Younger Children

Icy Breaths

Imagine you are blowing on a cold window.

Take in a deep breath, open your mouth and breathe out very slowly and steadily.

Can you see how misty the window is? Repeat this exercise.

This exercise is to help you control your out breath to help you feel relaxed.

Bubble Breaths

Imagine you are blowing bubbles of peace into the room.

Imagine you have a pot of bubble liquid. Take in a breath. Slowly and gently blow bubbles into the room.

As you blow out the bubbles, imagine they are filled with peace and the whole room is filling up with peace.
Do you feel peaceful?

This exercise is to help you use your breath and your imagination to become relaxed.

Index

activity systems 62–63
Adaptive Behaviour Assessment System 54
Adaptive Behaviour Scales 55
adrenaline response 1, 6
affective education 48, 83, 89
aggressive behaviours 7, 9, 20, 30, 39, 44, 84
agoraphobia 2
Albano, A. M. 51, 53
alcohol 9
alexithymia 17, 27, 28, 40, 55
American Psychiatric Association (APA) 1; *see also* Diagnostic and Statistical Manual (5th edition) (DSM-5)
anger management cards 120
Anxiety, Depression and Mood Scale (ADAMS) 52
Anxiety Disorders Interview Schedule-ASA (ADIS-ASA) 53, 54
Anxiety Disorders Interview Schedule-Child (ADIS-C) 51, 52, 53
Anxiety Disorders Interview Schedule-Child and Parent Version (ADIS-C/P) 53
Anxiety Scale for Children – ASD (ASC-ASD) 51, 53, 54
Ashton-Smith, J. 9
Asperger, H. 2
assessment of anxiety 48–57
attachment 9
auditory sensitivity 4, 42, 45, 59, 71
Ayres, A. J. 36

Baldwin, S. 9
Barendse, E. M. 28, 29
Baron-Cohen, S. 25
Beck, A. T. 52
Beck, J. S. 52
Beck Youth Inventories Second Edition for Children and Adolescents (BYI-II) 52
bed-wetting 9
Berthoz, S. 27
Birmaher, B. 52, 54
Black, K. R. 40
Blackburn, R. 14
Body Outline Worksheet 84
body scan 77, 107
Bogdashina, O. 12, 16, 21
break cards 86–87, 94
breathing techniques 74–75, 77, 97–105
Buhr, K. 4
bullying 19–20
Buron, K. D. 88
butterfly breaths 105

calm boxes 72–73
calm breaks 68–70, 88, 89, 94
calm breathing 74–75
calm corner tokens 95
calming strategies 72, 75–77, 90, 94–95; *see also* breathing techniques; relaxation
Carter, M. 64–65
Cath, D. C. 51
change as trigger 5, 26, 29–32, 51, 53, 65, 86, 89; Social Stories® 65; visual supports 62
Child and Adolescent Symptom Inventory (CASI-4) 51, 52, 53, 54
choice boards 59
Chorpita, B. F. 52, 53
co-regulation 89–90
Cognitive Behaviour Therapy (CBT) 78–82
cognitive coping cards 81–82
cognitive distortions 80
cognitive flexibility 9, 28, 29–32, 55
cognitive restructuring 80–81
colour coding: feelings 66; pens 87, 88; visual supports 124
comic strip conversations 65–66
communication 51, 86–89; cyclicity 21–22; differences 3, 12–24; management strategies 60–61; sensory input 43
compulsive behaviours 8; OCD 2, 51
coping strategies 6, 29–30, 60, 74, 81–82; *see also* management strategies
Costley, D. 9
criterion-referenced tests 50

Davis, T. 13, 17, 21
De Bruin, E. 75
depression 20, 30, 53
desensitisation 71–72
Diagnostic and Statistical Manual (5th edition) (DSM-5) 1, 12, 37–38
distraction techniques 79, 90
double empathy problem 25, 27–28
drugs 9
Dugas, M. J. 4
Dyck, M. J. 52

ear defenders 71
eating disorders 9, 10, 40
emotion book 85
emotion cards 86–87
emotion chart 111
emotion ladder 87–88
emotion speedometer 110
emotion thermometer 86, 87, 108–109
emotion traffic lights 87–88, 114
emotion volcano 88, 113
emotions: recognizing 83–85; regulation 55, 58, 72–73, 89–90

Esbensen, A. J. 52
executive functioning (EF) 4, 5, 25, 28–33, 34–35, 49
expressive language skills 3, 13, 15–17, 60, 86
externalisation of anxieties 7, 9
eye contact 43

familiarity 3, 5, 8, 31, 38, 43, 45–46, 66, 79
feelings *see* emotions
females with autism 9–10, 14, 18, 19–20, 86
fight, flight or freeze response 7–8, 19, 44–45, 47
flexibility 2, 60, 69; cognitive 9, 28, 29–32, 55
formal assessments 49–50
formal management strategies 61–73
friendships 12, 18, 19, 20–21
frustration 3, 6, 16, 32, 116–117

Gadow, K. D. 51, 54
gender 9–10, 14, 18, 19–20, 86
generalised anxiety disorder 3
goal setting 48, 50
Gould, J. 9
Grandin, T. 15, 34
Gray, C. 64, 65, 66
Green, S. A. 40
Greenhill, L. L. 51, 53
grounding activity 75, 76
group work 27, 59, 82
guided imagery 77

habituation 38
happiness switch 77
Harris, A. 15, 41
Harrison 55
Hartley, M. 75
help, asking for 4, 5, 17, 33, 48, 81, 118–119
Hill, E. L. 27
Hollocks, M. 28–29
home: calm breaks 68–69; flexibility 60; relaxation 74; returning from school 8, 44; stress kit 72
homework 5, 31, 32, 62
hyper-reactivity 4, 38–41, 43, 45–46, 79
hypo-reactivity 38, 39, 79

implicit learning 33
Incredible 5 Point Scale 87, 88
informal assessments 49, 50
inhibitory control 28
intelligence quotient (IQ) 49
internalisation of anxieties 7, 8, 9
International Classification of Diseases (11th edition) (ICD-11) 1
intolerance of uncertainty 4, 38, 40, 55
irrational fears 8

Jackson, L. 18
Johnson 21

Kanner, L. 2
Kendall, P. C. 3
Kerns, C. M. 3, 51, 53, 54
Klinger, L. G. 33
Knott, F. 1, 2, 52
Kreiser, N. 10, 14

Lawson, W. 29–30, 34
learning style *see* visual learning style
Lecavalier, L. 52
Lipsky, D. 8, 22
looks/sounds like rating scale 112
low arousal environments 66–68
low registration 39
Luna, B. 29

McAfee, J. 18
McConachie, H. 53
management strategies 58–92
March, J. S. 52, 54
Milton, D. 26–27
mindfulness 75–77
Multidimensional Anxiety Scale for Children (MASC) 52, 54
muscle relaxation 74, 96

National Institute for Clinical Excellence (NICE) 78–79
negative view/opinions 9
Neil, L. 4, 38, 40
neuropsychological measures 49
non-verbal communication 3, 12, 14–17, 83
noradrenaline 6
norm-referenced assessments 49

Oakland 54
obsessive-compulsive disorder (OCD) 2, 51
occupational therapy 59, 71
ocean breaths 103
Ozsivadjian, A. 1, 2, 51, 52, 54

Paediatric Anxiety Rating Scale (PARS) 51, 52, 53–54
panic disorder 3
Park, C. J. 13
Pearl, A. 52
peer awareness programmes 21
peer group work 82
Pellicano, E. 29
personal care tasks 8, 62–64
phobias 2, 40, 51
physiological responses 6–7, 17
Pickar, H. 21
planning skills 4, 5, 31, 32, 34
play 5, 26, 46, 55, 59, 63
A Poison Thought game 80, 81
pragmatic language skills 12
predictability/unpredictability 3–4, 5, 8, 17, 25, 27, 29–32, 38, 43, 46, 59, 61, 66, 90
Prizant, B. 27

proactive strategies 58, 66, 90
processing times 14, 15, 60
proprioceptive activities 70–71

rainbow breaths 104
reactive strategies 58
reassurance seeking 9
receptive language skills 3, 13, 14–15, 86
relaxation 59, 74–77, 96–105
repetitive behaviours 1, 8, 9, 14, 17, 46, 47, 51, 90
Revised Children's Anxiety and Depression Scale (RCADS) 51, 52, 53
Reynhout, G. 64–65
Ridderinkhof, E. 75
Riddle, M. A. 51, 53
Rodgers, J. 40, 41–42, 51, 53
role play 80, 85
routines 3, 5, 30, 45, 86

Samson, A. 27
school attendance/school refusal 1, 8, 14, 20, 31
school specific anxieties 5–6, 19–20, 32, 34
Screen for Child Anxiety Related Emotional Disorders (SCARED) 52, 53, 54
self-esteem 16, 82, 89
self harm 9, 46–47
self prompt regulation cards 88–89
self-regulation 27, 37, 82
self-report 51, 52, 55
self-talk 81–82
sensory avoidance 45
sensory defensiveness 44
sensory integration theory 36
sensory overload 4, 37–38, 43, 70
sensory processing 4, 36–47
sensory seeking 39
sensory stimuli 5, 42–43, 61, 66, 86
sensory systems 36, 42
separation anxiety disorder 3
Sharma, S. 25
shut down 8, 39, 45
Silverman, W. K. 51, 53
sleep disturbances 9
Smyth-Myles, B. 50
social anxiety 2, 17–21, 51
social avoidance 16, 19, 20, 40, 51
social awareness 9
social cognition 17
social demands 5
Social Stories® 59, 64–65, 85
social withdrawal and isolation 3, 7, 8, 21, 43, 48
South, M. 40, 41–42
Sparrow, S. S. 55
speech 21, 43
Spence Children's Anxiety Scale (SCAS) 52, 53, 54
Spence, S. H. 52, 54
Sprafkin, J. 51, 54
square breathing 101
Stallard, P. 79
standardised assessments 49
star breathing 102
Stern, J. A. 54
Storch, E. A. 53
story-based interventions 64–65
stress hormones *see* adrenaline response; noradrenaline
stress kits 72–73
structure 5, 20, 59; conversations 21; structured tasks 63–64; structured teaching 35, 61–64
Sukhodolsky, D. G. 54
sympathetic nervous system 6–7
tactile sensitivity 4, 40, 42–43, 44, 45, 46, 71

Tantam, D. 21
TEACCH model 33, 35, 61–64
Theory of Mind (ToM) 25–28, 34–35
transitions 5, 26–27, 30–31, 46, 59
Trembath, D. 51
triggers 5–9, 41–44, 47; identifying 86, 89; management strategies 58, 59–60; removal 59–60; *see also* change as trigger

Uljarevic, M. 40, 41
Ung, D. 53

Van Steensel, F. J. A. 2
Vineland Adaptive Behaviour Scales 55
visual learning style 25, 33–35
visual schedules 61–62, 93
visual supports 60–65, 75, 84–85, 87, 90, 124
visual timetables 59
visualisation 77

Wechsler Individual Achievement Test 55
weighted items 70–71
Weisz, J. 77
White, S. 10, 14, 25, 53
Wigham, S. 53
Williams, D. 17
Wilson, J. M. 17
Wing, L. 16
Wintgens 21
Wood, J. J. 54
working memory 28, 29
World Health Organisation (WHO) 1

younger children 122–123

For Product Safety Concerns and Information please contact our EU representative GPSR@taylorandfrancis.com Taylor & Francis Verlag GmbH, Kaufingerstraße 24, 80331 München, Germany

* 9 7 8 0 3 6 7 2 5 0 3 3 1 *

T - #0023 - 260226 - C138 - 297/210/6 - SB - 9780367250331 - Gloss Lamination